THE COLOR OF A LION'S EYE

To Frank Wade
who
set my feet on
the path

Thanks so much,

Jane Bonin

ALSO BY JANE F. BONIN

Prize Winning American Drama: A Bibliographical and Descriptive Guide

Mario Fratti (Twayne's World Authors Series)

Major Themes in Prizewinning American Drama

THE COLOR OF A LION'S EYE:

Memories of Africa

Jane F. Bonin

Library of Congress Control Number: 2015942370

ISBN: 978-0-9862801-6-0

Printed in the United States

Cover design by Martin W. Romero

TABLE OF CONTENTS

DEDICATED TO

Diane Marquart Moore and Victoria I. Sullivan without whom this work would never have seen the light of day and to Wynn Creasy who provided constant encouragement and support

PREFACE

For six years the continent of Africa was my home. From 1994 until 1996, I held the position of Associate Peace Corps Director in Malawi. Near the end of that two-year hitch, I was appointed Peace Corps County Director of Niger; a position I held until the end of my tour when I returned to the United States in 2000.

I was not a typical Peace Corps staffer. I had a PhD in English Literature. I had spent years in the academic world as professor and advisor. I had been wife, mother, and grandmother. After a divorce I took early retirement from university teaching. I moved to Washington, DC, and worked as a federal employee at the US State Department, before looking for a new challenge with the Peace Corps. I had never been a Peace Corps Volunteer in Africa or anywhere else. I knew nothing of Africa except what I imagined. In an attempt to convince the Peace Corps Director in Washington to hire me, I went on vacation to Senegal, my first footfall on the African continent.

Africa hit my bloodstream like a powerful drug. My mother had suffered from migraine headaches, and her description of their onset was suddenly understandable: more color, more contrast, more noise, and fewer defenses against the intensity of the incoming stimuli. I was dazed and dazzled by the vibrancy of what I saw, smelled, and felt. I was scammed out of 100 US dollars within the first twenty-four hours in the country. Even that seemed amazing, and I've dined out on the story for years.

By the time I took my post in Malawi, I still in a kind of altered state. Everything in Africa seemed exaggerated—my pale hands against the dark hands I shook, the smells of spicy food frying in the streets, the music blaring from every shop doorway, the blinding glare of the sun. I never smoked Malawi Gold, reputed to be some of the most desirable marijuana in the world, but I felt as if I had. Africa was a six-year drugless high with no social or legal consequences and no hangover. Nothing in my life has been as intense or as exciting as my time there. I learned a lot, some of which I wish I could forget. My heart cracked every day, and the ways I tried to paper it over enough to get my job done were not always effective. It was an overwhelming time from which I have not recovered and perhaps don't want to.

This account is not a scholarly or journalistic analysis of African life and culture. Nor is it a discussion of the Peace Corps, an organization I admire and was privileged to serve. It is rather an effort to set down a few vignettes, hoping they might convey something of the extraordinary things I saw and felt during those years. I want to remember and share those moments I was privileged to have. The essays and thoughts that follow are an attempt to pull together some disparate threads of my six years serving those who serve in that place of astonishing and terrible beauty. I have set down what seems worth retelling with all the accuracy and clarity I can muster.

If we were in Africa we would sit on a mat under a tree and tell our stories one to the other. I hope this remembrance will be the next best thing.

BEGINNINGS

I WENT TO AFRICA KNOWING that I wanted to make life better for African people, but having little understanding of how I would do it. I accepted a staff job with The US Peace Corps in Malawi without knowing exactly where Malawi was.

I grew up in the Jim Crow South in the forties and fifties, and even as a child I felt blistering shame at the racial injustices of a system so hideous that even a young person could not escape seeing them. Black people were an intimate part of most southern households. They cooked our food, minded our children, nursed our sick, and often lived under the same roof or on the same property—on the place—as people say in the South. I loved so many of them and was sad and angry to witness their plight but felt helpless to make anything different for them.

Even my grandparents, who toiled their whole lives through on behalf of blacks, were casually racist. My grandmother told the black children that they could only play with my brother and me if they went home to wash up and change clothes. This from a woman who knew they had no running water in their miserable little shacks. Both my grandparents referred to black people as "Niggras," which was considered polite in those days.

I felt myself small and powerless in these situations. I couldn't say anything without offending my grandparents, whom I loved and knew to be kind and caring people. I consoled myself with the thought that someday, when I was a big person, I would do something to improve their lot.

When I look back on my choice to work for the Peace Corps, I don't have to look far to see the roots of a strong imperative to serve others. All four of my grandparents had college degrees in the nineteenth century, something of a rarity. My people on both sides served. There was not a single businessman or entrepreneur among the dozens of ministers, doctors, nurses, teachers, and social workers.

On my mother's side, the ranks were thick with pastors. Her father, Harry Goodwin Knowles, was a fiery preacher who began his ministry as a Campbellite circuit rider serving multiple congregations on the plains of Nebraska. I have a photograph of him on a huge motorcycle with my grandmother, Lavinia Cox, riding shotgun in a sidecar, holding one of her five babies.

According to family mythology, he single-handedly stopped a lynching in Little Rock, Arkansas, by demanding that the perpetrators kneel and pray, or suffer the consequences. He was a man who attracted stories like this, but I myself saw the medal that the Governor of Arkansas presented to him for quelling that mob. That he was later chaplain of the Houston, Texas Police Force seemed fitting. Short and stocky, with a big chest and heavily muscled arms, he had been a boxer in his youth and was certainly no sissified pastor.

I remember him in his mellow years when he was the beloved pastor of a large downtown church in Houston. Known also as The Radio Pastor, his voice boomed out to a large audience each week, and thanks to the clear-channel station in the area, his broadcasts could be heard all over Texas and parts of Mexico.

He was the most public person in my family, a civic leader with a reputation as a masterful preacher devoted to Ecumenism, and something of a left-leaning anti-segregationist, or a "pinko nigger-lover," as his detractors would have it.

My grandfather on my father's side, Henry Milburn Faust, was a country doctor who spent his career working in the obscurity of rural Louisiana. He seemed gruff to me, and I didn't know him well. He was often away for days at a time; first, in a horse and buggy, later in a Model T. He wound his way up and down the muddy bayous, treating everyone, black and white alike. There were no other doctors nearby, no dentists, and no hospitals in this barren area. He did it all. He only came home after the fever had broken, the baby had been delivered, the bone had been set, or the patient had passed to the realm beyond his help. He was rarely and poorly paid. Sometimes his compensation came home with him—perhaps a piglet, if his patient were prosperous, a chicken or a bucket of pecans if not. Mostly he returned with nothing, but that was never mentioned, at least within my earshot.

No one in my family on either side seemed to care much about money. This spirit was strikingly exemplified by my father's three uncles—Uncle Will, Uncle Walter, and Uncle Alex. They went together to the Draft Board to decline the pension that President Truman awarded to Veterans of World War I. They declared that they had not expected more money. They were proud to have served their country and were happy to have returned alive and unscathed. Besides that, they would probably otherwise never have seen Paris.

Likewise, my grandmother Faust, born Martha Smith and known as Miss Mattie, taught the local children of all ages in the one-room schoolhouse she had established on the Faust property. She continued to teach during the Depression after the State of Louisiana could only pay in "script." She kept these worthless pieces of paper in a cigar box in her armoire (her "chifferobe," she called it), knowing they would probably never be redeemed. When I asked her why she worked for nothing, she shrugged and said that the children needed to be taught.

I myself was a teacher by training and profession. I married a successful lawyer, had two children, and earned the obligatory PhD. I wrote the obligatory books that allowed me to teach English at the University level for twenty pleasant years.

For most of those years, the seventies, eighties, and part of the nineties, I worked as a volunteer in hunger relief organizations. I was honed on that grindstone. My job was to raise money and consciousness about the prevalence and gravity of hunger in the world. The training and the work were rigorous. It was like a second, full-time job. I would later use, in my role as Peace Corps Director, all the skills that I had acquired–fundraising, briefing, and managing volunteers, creating and supporting commitment.

I loved working on hunger issues. I learned to play on teams, one of which, a group of seven, raised a million dollars in six months' time. These successes were satisfying, but I had a growing sense that my work was too indirect, too abstract. It was just talking. I wanted to confront poverty, malnutrition, disease, and illiteracy face-to-face in the field. I wanted to be on that line.

That I was ill suited to this purpose seems to have escaped my notice. I had no training for what I wanted to do, not even rudimentary first-aid. I was squeamish and sentimental. My romantic vision of binding wounds and spooning soup to the parched lips of the sick and starving ended, predictably perhaps, in a humiliating dark night of the soul.

Reality set in when I decided to join a local physician who made regular trips to Lima, Peru, to work in one of Mother Theresa's hospitals. I had heard of his expeditions through my next-door neighbor whose cousin had been a volunteer on one of his missions. He often took volunteers along, so I signed up to go during the summer vacation from the University.

A month or so before we were scheduled to leave, he invited the group of about twenty-five volunteers to his house for a spaghetti supper and orientation. Many of these people had gone with him before and were seasoned veterans. I was just putting my toe into the water they had been swimming in for years.

After supper had been cleared, we sat around the table while he spoke. He was a stern-looking man who reminded the group that they could not expect much support from him, as he would be in surgery most of the time. Neither he nor the hospital staff was going to baby-sit us. We must find ways to make ourselves useful. How I would do that with no Spanish and no nursing skills, I couldn't imagine; but I was full of ungrounded optimism and delusions of competence in those days.

After a brief discussion about the logistics of the

trip, he took a few questions and then began projecting a slide show upon the dining room wall. That good man must have intended the pictures to discourage the uncommitted or faint-hearted, for they spared nothing. I was unprepared for what I saw—the appalling slums of Lima with the jumble of shacks, the animals in the street, the ragged children, the occasional cripples dragging themselves on crutches or on all-fours.

Then the focus shifted to the hospital, another shock. I had assumed that it would be calm and quiet, with the lovely sisters in their characteristic blue and white saris, firmly in charge of a peaceful healing environment.

Instead, I saw images of rotting flesh, maggoty wounds, glittering, feverish eyes, grotesquely twisted limbs, cleft palates, and amputations. I felt faint and ill; and after only twenty-minutes, I slipped out and vomited my spaghetti into the bushes.

I scarcely remember driving home, and what followed was a terrible night. I was exhausted, but sleep would not come. When I closed my eyes, those horrific images assailed me. One in particular was the most tormenting, as if seared to the underside of my eyelids: an emaciated young woman holding a tiny baby to her flaccid breast. She was staring without expression at the dead or dying child, too exhausted to brush away the flies clustered on its motionless eyes.

For most of the night, I was wracked with revulsion, rage, and despair. I wasn't who I thought I was. I couldn't become who I wanted to be. I had no skills. I had no guts. I could not serve. I would be throwing up in the shrubbery while others were helping the sick. I was nothing but an ineffectual do-gooder. Never in my life had I felt such blistering shame.

At the height of this agitation, I heard these

words: "Serve those who serve." They rang in my ears like little crystal bells. Around first light, a sweet calm settled around me, and finally I slept for the rest of the night and for most of the next day. I had my marching orders.

ARRIVING

I KNEW I WOULD GO to Africa, but I found my way there by a less-than-direct route. I realized that I needed to retrain myself and to put myself in an environment where people did international work.

During my tenure as a university professor I had worked intensely with various hunger response organizations. That work took me away from my family, causing turmoil at home, especially with my husband, who was not enthusiastic about this second life I was creating for myself. I was also inspired by the great wave of feminist anger breaking at that time. It allowed me to think that being my own person was a legitimate goal. Few women in our circle worked at that time or pursued any interest that did not fit snugly into family life; so even my going back to school and teaching was something of an embarrassment to my family. I was not particularly smart or subtle about the way I pursued the freedom to be the kind of person I wanted to be. I tended to view any disapproval or objection as old-fashioned oppression.

Following the inevitable divorce, I bought a little cottage near the university and began establishing my independence. Why not? My children were grown. My husband and I had grown apart. I felt I was ready for a leap into the unknown.

After a few more years, I left my tenured professorship, sold my cottage for less than I paid for it, pulled up my taproot, and moved to Washington, DC, without a job.

I went to work with a small consulting firm that served mostly public sector clients. After a year or so, I was hired by the Foreign Service Institute to manage part of their system for delivering training to new and seasoned diplomats. At FSI, I had colleagues who had been country directors for the Peace Corps. As a result of their encouragement I applied for a position with the Peace Corps. At my initial interview, I was informed that I could not be awarded a country directorship as I had never set foot on African soil, I had not been a Peace Corps Volunteer, and I didn't know the culture of the organization—all the objections I had voiced in my own mind.

I coolly informed her that I already had a trip planned to Senegal in the next three weeks. I called up a friend, and we made this little white lie a reality.

When I returned after my trip she seemed duly impressed and asked me what kind of job I wanted. I heard myself saying, "I want a job so big that I'm scared when I wake up in the morning." The director said, dryly, "I think we can fix you up." And indeed, they did.

I was offered a position as the Programming and

Training officer in Malawi. Not a directorship, but a position that included the duties and responsibilities of the second-in-command.

When I try to remember arriving in Malawi, my strongest recollection was of a country burning down. As we circled, waiting to land, I looked out the windows. The billowing smoke, tongues of flame, and the blackened scorched earth, made it appear the whole countryside was on fire. The rather pleasant smell of smoke hit my nostrils even before I walked down the steps to the tarmac. I later learned that Malawians have a practice of burning off the stubble from their fields in preparation for the next planting of corn. The sugarcane farmers do the same thing in Louisiana, but I remember it as a more controlled exercise.

The airport seemed disorderly to me, not as chaotic as the one in Dakar but unsettling to a newcomer. I felt I was entering a strange and mysterious realm. I was a white stranger amid a sea of Africans. I didn't know Bobbye, the Country Director, who was picking me up; but getting through the paperwork and luggage inspection was a slow process, and I fretted that she had probably been waiting a long time. I didn't know then that waiting was a way of life in Africa. When I emerged into the public area, there she was, looking expectantly at me. "Dr. Bonin, I presume." We both laughed at the little joke, and she presented me to a Malawian in a jumpsuit wearing a Peace Corps pin on his collar. She let him deal with the baggage while we went out and climbed into the white SUV with the Peace Corps emblem on the door.

I liked Bobbye at once. She was a tiny, pretty woman with an angelic face and clouds of white-blond hair. We went to her huge, rambling house, where she installed me in one of the many guest rooms. That night, I met Weston, the cook, and Katie, the

Weimaraner. They would both become fixtures in my life after Bobbye finished her tour of duty in the next few weeks and returned to the States. Weston bowed slightly and said, "Welcome, Madame. We are happy you have come." Katie greeted me by getting up on the sofa beside me, looking expectantly into my eyes, and putting her big paws on my lap.

During dinner, Bobbye suggested that I leave the next day to go to the twelve-week Pre-Service Training for the newly-arrived class which was in progress. Since my job was managing all the training in the Malawi program, I was glad to get a look at an important piece.

It was cold during the night, and I got up and rummaged through my luggage for a pair of socks. The next morning when I walked into the large bathroom with its highly polished tile floors, my feet slipped out from under me and I hit my head. I lay on the floor trying to assess the damage and thinking that this wasn't how I wanted to enter my new life. I felt sheepish telling Bobbye of my accident. Even though I minimized the pain in my head and neck, she insisted that we stop in to see the Post Medical Officer. Nana, a beautiful young woman from Guinea, checked me out and gave me a handful of painkillers, which I didn't take.

I went the next day to The Grace Bandawe Training Center in Blantyre, the commercial capital of Malawi. The training center was named for Dr. Livingston's birthplace in Scotland. When I was introduced as the next Director for Programming and Training, the trainees and staff all eyed me curiously. I saw them through a haze of fatigue. I was going into a steep decline from jet lag and the seventeen-hour trip that even a night in Bobbye's comfortable bed had not erased. We had arrived at the center at teatime. I had weak tea and several biscuits and begged off supper. I didn't want to nod off in my plate. I went to my room as soon as decently possible, fell asleep instantly, and slept through the night without turning over.

Early the next morning, I was awakened by the unmistakable sounds of African women laughing and the scent of wood smoke. Through the window, I saw a group behind the training center. All of them were clad in bright, primary colored lengths of fabric in various geometric patterns. They wore them tied around their waists; some also tied up their hair with the same fabrics. They were gathered around three timpani-sized iron wash pots simmering over small open fires. Some stirred the clothes in the water with sticks, some scrubbed them on metal washboards, and some rinsed them in a separate pot and hung them on lines to dry. They laughed and chattered while at these labors. Even though they were speaking *Chichewa* and I couldn't understand a word, nothing about this picture seemed foreign to me. While visiting my grandmother's house in a tiny rural hamlet in Louisiana, I had seen this scene many times before. I felt instantly at home.

SETTLING IN

AFTER A COUPLE OF DAYS, I recovered from the
seventeen-hour flight, and Bobbye was able to give me
a lot of her time to teach me the job. She was careful
to see that I had been properly instructed and
introduced. She presented me to the important people
both at the Embassy and in the Malawi Government
Ministries. We also traveled around the country to
meet Volunteers. We found that we liked each other
and had fun together. I knew I would miss her after
she left.

Shortly after I arrived, she sent me with a car and
driver to the training site. I was an advocate of village-
based training, but at the time of my arrival the
trainees were still being trained under a model called
Center-Based Training at the Grace Bandawe Centre,
in Lilongwe, the capital of Malawi.

Instead of staying at the Centre, I was lodged with a middle-class Malawian family by the name of Nyasulu. I ate every meal at the Nyasulu's table with them and their son Ish (short for Ishmael). Their welcome was warm and generous, and I felt safe and contented in their care. I would go back to them several more times to supervise the ninety trainees and try to solve as many problems as I could.

Before his retirement, Bambo (Father) Nyasulu had been a clinical officer in the health ministry, a mid-level civil servant. Amayi (Mother) spoke no English, but we communicated very effectively in the universal language of women.

On the morning after my arrival, she managed to convey to me that she would prepare my bath. She heated the water in a pot over a three-stone fire, then poured it into a large plastic tub and set it in the bath house, a small outbuilding with a concrete floor in the family compound. After I bathed, I wanted to empty the water, but she insisted otherwise. I protested, until Bambo told me that it was her job and her pleasure to serve me. She had also placed a *pot de chambre* under the bed to use at night. I absolutely refused to have her empty my slops, and so I always went out to the privy in back, even though I was afraid I would encounter snakes or spiders.

The first full day of my visit, Bambo placed a small table and two chairs on the *khande*. I sat there every day, all day, consulting with a steady stream of volunteers, trainees, trainers, and training staff.

When it was time to go, Mr. Nyasulu said sadly, "And now you will shut up your office and leave us." I said, "Yes, Bambo. But I will be coming back, if you will have me." He said, "Amayi and I will welcome you at any time."

Bobbye was wise to put me up with the Nyasulus. During the next training cycle, the trainees would live mostly in the bush and in villages with Malawian families, eat their food, sleep in their beds, and bathe in their buckets. They would be impressed that I had gone before them and had not stayed at Grace Bandawe as training directors had done in the past.

When I got back to Lilongwe from my introduction to the bush, my job at the Peace Corps office had already started and was in full swing.

The person I was replacing, a young woman named Carla, would be leaving in two or three weeks. The plan was for me to remain at Bobbye's until Carla's departure, at which time I would take over both her job and her house.

When I met with Carla so she could show me the house and talk about the job I was about to inherit, I asked her if she had any regrets now that she was preparing to move on. We were at the time of this conversation sitting on the spacious veranda of the house. She waved her hand and said, "I wish I had taken time to enjoy all of this."

The "all of this" included the *khande*, a broad, intensely green lawn which swept two-hundred feet to the road. This astonishing lawn was dotted with six or seven flame trees and several jacarandas, giving one the image of an impressionist painting composed of impossible colors, deep blue-green expanses with splashes of brilliant fiery orange and cool purple.

Also included in the "all this" was the low-slung, rambling house which contained nine or ten large rooms, as well as spacious corridors and the large veranda we were enjoying at the moment. Out back was a large vegetable garden tended by Carla's gardener named Kennedy. The back yard also included servants' quarters and outbuildings used for storage and tools.

From the veranda we could see Mt. Mulanje, the highest mountain in Malawi, thrusting itself up from the gently undulating plain and soaring to a height of three thousand feet. It was a cloudy, smoky day. Malawian farmers were still burning off their fields so I couldn't see the top of the mountain, which I had been told had snow on it for much of the year.

I could imagine living on this place, the largest home I would ever have enjoyed. I would be mistress of the manor. Sharing the place with me would be Bobbye's admirable employee Weston, whom I hired as cook and house worker at her departure. He and his family, consisting of a wife and four children, would be moving into the servants' quarters. Kennedy, I retained as gardener after Carla's departure. Katie the dog would also be a member of this new group and would join us after Bobbye left.

Carla's expression of regret returned to me many times during my two years in Malawi, reminding me to be conscious of beauty and pleasure even when the workload was onerous.

While I was still camped out at Bobbye's, an issue arose over the accommodations for Weston and his family. When he saw the dwelling where Carla's worker, Flatware, had lived, he promptly declared it unacceptable. It was a compact, two-room dwelling with cement floors; too small for a family of six, too dark, too primitive, and without indoor plumbing. Bobbye gave orders for the speedy renovation of the house and outbuildings. Neither she nor I would allow it to be called by the local designation, "Boys' Quarters." I often wondered how Weston's children had felt when they heard their home referred to in that way, implying that their dignified forty-five year-old father was a mere "boy." I assumed that the British colonizers saw that calling grown black and brown men "boys" was one of the many ways of keeping them in a perpetual state of inferiority. The French were guilty too. I once read that among the colonizing French a waiter's white coat was known as a *jacket de boy*. France had only recently stopped calling a skilled professional waiter *Garçon*.

When Weston's quarters were finished to his satisfaction, I finally moved into the big house. Weston, his tiny wife Miriam, and their four children: Monica, then fourteen; Jeff, nine; Dave, eight; and the baby, Helen, joined me on the place.

I loved having them around, watching them come and go to school in their spotless uniforms, watching the little boys play with their homemade toys, seeing the baby toddle about, hearing their lilting voices through the kitchen windows. Weston told me how happy the children were that I had come. One of his former employers, a British couple, had forbidden them to appear near the house or to be seen on the grounds. They were permitted to use the driveway when going to school; otherwise, they were to stay out of sight and hearing of the house. Now they were happy because they had the run of the lawn to play their games, roll their hoops, and, in the evening, catch fireflies.

Once installed in the freshly painted house, I was completely at home. I had inherited the government-issue faux Queen Anne furniture and the Embassy "Welcome Kit," a set of plastic dishes and battered, stainless flatware intended to tide newcomers over until their personal effects arrived.

The United States Government or USG, as it was routinely called among government employees, handled overseas moves by personnel in three stages. First, one brought one's carry-on baggage, with enough clothes and personal items to last for about a week. Next, came the airfreight. This shipment was more generous, including more clothes and personal items. The third installment of everything else— furnishings, household linens, kitchen necessities, table service, books, etc., would come by sea and could take months to arrive. Thus, I would not have to concern myself with organization and decor until a later time. There would be time for all that.

After the rigors of preparing to move overseas I found this time one of peace and liberation. Unlike many of my colleagues who were anxious for their stuff, I felt no urgency about my own. I drifted about the house that was not mine, furnished with things I would not have chosen, and felt a delightful detachment from domestic chores. I bought vases at the market and filled them with the flowers that Malawi offered in such abundance—from the garden, from the flowering trees, and from the sides of the roads where they grew wild in profusion.

One aspect of overseas life that I had to get used to was being guarded twenty-four hours a day. I had seen guards around Bobbye's place. I never realized that my own house would have guards; but there they were from the first moment I arrived. I wasn't happy when I realized that I would never be alone again. I would never be able sit on the *khande* by myself. Nudity, of course, was out of the question. I had been told that life on the Peace Corps staff would mean living in a fishbowl. When I heard that, I thought it meant "don't get drunk, smoke dope, beat your dog, or have lovers spending the night." It was worse than that. I felt it meant the end of any personal solitude. I would have to make a serious adjustment to the fishbowl.

The guards, without which no *mzungu* household was complete, formed a large part of the work force in Malawi. I suspect they were less than useful in deterring crime, as they were unarmed; but the job gave men who would otherwise be unemployed something to do. The guard changed at 6 in the morning and again at 6 in the evening. At dawn and around dusk they were visible everywhere on the roads, coming from or going to work.

Three guard companies work on contract in Lilongwe: Securicorp, the company the Peace Corps employs; Team 5, the company the Embassy contracts; and Force 1.

Securicorp guards were a holdover from British colonial times. They wore trim green uniforms with officer's caps. They did some funny little stamping footwork and saluted when I drove through the gate or when they came to the door for any reason. If I called one of them, he invariably responded, "Madam?"

The Team 5 guards wore grey uniforms and cream-colored berets. As part of the American Embassy Security program, they also had their own little dance and salute.

The oddest, however, were the Force 1 guys, who sported black fatigues with riot helmets, the kind with plastic visors. They guarded the universally despised but very wealthy Indian population. The Indians were ghettoized in my neighborhood, so I saw Force 1 guards often. They were dressed to look quite sinister, thanks to too much American TV, I suspect.

Guards were strictly forbidden to sleep on the job, but they all did. Maybe that was why it was customary to have two on duty at night: one could nap while the other kept the watch. Both of mine slept all night long. I gave them their tea around 6:30 or 7, and they sacked out shortly after. I didn't see them again unless I happened to startle them by turning on the kitchen light after they thought I was down for the night. If they heard or saw me, they roused up, coughed conspicuously, and made a show of patrolling the perimeter. We were instructed to report them to headquarters if we caught them sleeping, but I didn't feel strongly enough to do anything. The guards had so little money that most of them had day jobs just to make ends meet. Many worked eighty-ninety hour weeks. If I had thought that their presence prevented burglary or if I had been paying for their services myself, I might have felt more strongly.

Their presence was not reassuring to me; and in fact, they weighed on my conscience. When I sat down to my supper I was aware that I was eating a three-course meal while the guards were outside sitting on their haunches and getting by on bread and tea. I often went to the store for their bread and jam when I wouldn't have gone for myself. A couple of times a week and always on Sunday, I served them cookies and buttered their bread.

I never got used to their constant presence. I worried about them if they coughed or if their trousers looked loose. The HIV-Aids epidemic was worsening, and the guard force had already been hit hard. My time in Malawi was before retro-viral medications were available, so an HIV-Aids infection was a certain death sentence.

The stress of never being alone in my own home, the pressure of work in the office, and the responsibility for the lives of the volunteers and trainees under my direction made me long for the simplicity and comfort of the times spent with the Nyasulus.

When my own family came the next year to visit, I sent word to the Nyasulus that I would appreciate the opportunity for my children and grandchildren to greet them and asked if I could bring them for a visit. They agreed, and we set off for the bush. Weston had prepared a feast for us to share with them, and we all ate together around their table. It was a warm and lovely time. When we were getting ready to leave, Ish came forward, holding a protesting chicken toward me with outstretched arms. "Put it in the vehicle,"

Bambo instructed. We rode back to Lilongwe with the chicken, one of the ugliest and scrawniest I had ever seen, hopping and squawking and crapping all the way home.

When Weston came out to welcome us home, I told him the chicken was his for the taking. He knew just what to do with it and reported later that it was tough but tasty. I had been told that to be given a chicken was a great honor. I hoped I had received it with the same dignity with which it was proffered.

The Nyasulus were the first Malawians I loved, and there would be many more to come.

THE HELIOCENTRIC WORLD

AFTER MOVING TO MALAWI, I went to bed earlier than I ever had in my life. Sometimes when friends called from the States around 9 or 10 my time, I was already asleep. Whereas I had once gotten along fine on five or six hours of sleep and seven hours was a long night, after settling in Africa I routinely got eight or nine. Many of the Volunteers lived in houses without electricity, so going to bed when dark came made sense. Furthermore, Africans had no concept of keeping quiet so as not to disturb others. In villages, people all got up at first light. Roosters ensured that no one slept past 5 a.m.

But even the Volunteers who lived in town and had lights went to bed early. In Lilongwe, there was little to do after dark. The city was spread out, so there was no community nightlife, no place to stroll and stop in for a little cappuccino and jazz, or catch a movie and have a burger afterward.

The only time I went out at night was to have dinner with friends or to attend official functions (real command performances.) These events usually started early, so one could get home by bedtime at 9. When I drove home from these events I noticed that the town looked like places in the U.S. at 3 in the morning—absolutely no traffic, no noise, nothing open.

Going to bed so early made getting up early much easier. Since I had been for many years an early riser, (a habit formed when I was going to graduate school), I rather liked the rhythm. Mornings in Africa were gorgeous—fresh and cool and quiet. I usually ran before the dogs woke up and started barking and before the changing of the guard. After 6, the guards were all over the roads. *Azungu* (in Chichewa, the plural term for white people) running around in little shorts excited their interest, sometimes their obvious disapproval.

CONTRASTS

I WENT TO AFRICA, AMONG other reasons, to see if I could do some good in the world, support a purpose that, as Shaw put it, I "recognize to be a mighty one." Looking after that agenda took me from 6:30 in the morning until 6:30 or later in the evening, with official duties at night three or four times a week, and stints as the duty officer for a week at a time every three weeks. (We were only three Americans, with a Malawian staff of twenty. The three of us—Vyrle, Paul, and I—rotated the duty among ourselves. Having the duty meant being on call twenty-four hours a day in the event there was any emergency (and with eighty-six Volunteers in the country, crises were frequent and inevitable). We didn't take morning or afternoon coffee breaks although Steven, one of our porters, brought tea around 10 a.m., or "half ten," as they said in Africa. The dimensions of the job were staggering; although I characteristically put in ten-, sometimes twelve-or even fourteen-hour days, I was never through with my work, sometimes just barely ahead of whatever was snapping at my heels. I began to realize that any part of my job—Volunteer support, for example, or staff development, or reporting to Washington could become a regular eight-hour job if done properly and imaginatively.

When I got home, the picture changed—because I had Weston. In another place in the world, Weston would have been an artist, a master chef, a caterer of fancy dinners and parties. How I was lucky enough to get him I don't know. I knew from Bobbye that he was a better-than-average Malawian servant, used to working for *azungu*. She said he was honest, loyal, and never asked for loans (which the others did routinely).

What I didn't expect was the quality of his caretaking and the refinement of his sensibility. He intuited what I wanted and needed and simply produced it. For example, I mentioned during his first week with me that I loved having a garden with many flowers. After I made this remark, he put fresh bouquets in my bedroom and the study every few days. They were real Malawian medleys, compositions of colors and textures that I would never have thought of putting together, but when Weston did the arrangements, they looked natural, charming.

When we had our talk about what I wanted him to do, I asked him to have breakfast ready by 6 a.m. When he discovered that I got up and made coffee first thing, he started coming in before I was up to put on the pot. He was never in the kitchen when I stumbled in at 5 or so, but the coffee was always fresh and hot. He showed up again around "half five" and did breakfast, which he set out on the *khande* so I didn't have to talk.

When I first hired him, I had the idea that I would tell him every day what I wanted to eat for lunch and dinner and what to serve when I planned to have company. As soon as I got really busy at the office, he started preparing meals according to what was in the fridge and the garden. If he needed something, he went to the Hyperstore on his bike and got it. When I arrived home, he set it out very nicely—place mat, cloth napkin, covered serving dishes with serving utensils. I ate whatever he put before me. It was always good, albeit sometimes a little strange. He made chicken salad with carrots, bell peppers, and onions. Unexpected, but nice.

When we had company, I involved myself a little more. I told him how many guests would come, and he told me what we could have, then I selected something. If I forgot to mention dessert, he simply cooked one. He served the table impeccably, made a good gin-and-tonic, passed the coffee tray when he sensed that it was time for the dinner to be over.

At first, being served at this level made me feel guilty—all this for one person. But I must say truthfully that I was soon into the routine. I told myself that I couldn't put in the kind of day I normally did without the level of support he provided. I knew this was mostly rationalization, "BS," actually; but it worked for me. I also reminded myself that this wouldn't last forever and I'd be back to schlepping my own groceries and eating breakfast standing up before too long. Still, I considered it some kind of cosmic irony that the more I tried to do good in the world, the more I lived like a princess.

LE CHANGEMENT DU REGIME

A WEEK OR SO BEFORE Bobbye was to leave, she moved into my house so the new director, Vyrle, could move into her place. She arrived with Katie, her gorgeous Weimaraner, and a pair of cats with two newborn kittens. The long-awaited Weston and Miriam, together with their four children, were finally installed in newly renovated lodgings on the grounds. As soon as I could find a home for the felines, I was happy to let them go. Cute as they were, they didn't inspire me to keep them, even with Weston there to look after them. The first time one of them pooped in my favorite picnic basket, all of them went to a family who needed some good *mausers*. The cats were not fancy animals, like Katie, whose pedigree cited her ancestors as Baron von This and Baroness von That.

These cats were simple barn cats that would *maus* up the place in short order, I assumed.

Gradually, the household staff settled in place: Weston and family, Kennedy the gardener, and the guards—a day guard and two night guards. I found it a sobering responsibility to have ten people on the place. I was expected not only to pay them, but also to take charge if any of their children fell ill. They would look to me to take them to the hospital and to pay for their medicine. I knew a Volunteer whose guard died. She paid for his funeral, his casket, and the transport for the funeral party to his distant village in the north, her living allowance for several months. There was no social safety net out there. I thought of these people as my opportunity to act locally instead of just thinking globally, which I could do rather well but which costs nothing. I hoped that I could leave them better off than I found them. I also hoped it wouldn't cost too much.

Another concern was Katie. Shortly after Bobbye departed, she began to fail, crying and whimpering at night, refusing food and scratching herself raw in the daytime. I took her to a veterinarian who said he couldn't find anything wrong with her. He gave her a huge vitamin shot and suggested that maybe she had worms, or maybe she had an allergy to fleas, etc. It was clear to me that he had no idea what to do. After I brought her back home, she got steadily worse. The next night, when I came home late from an official function at the Embassy, she made an attempt to stand up but staggered and fell, her eyes fixed and glassy, her breathing shallow and rapid.

I decided she probably wouldn't last the night, so I made her a bed on the *khande.* I figured it would be easier to dispose of her body if she were outside the house rather than in the house. The practical side of my nature surprises me from time to time.

While I sat beside her, I had the realization that she wasn't sick but was grieving herself to death for Bobbye, and that she had some choice in the matter. I put my lips close to her ear and whispered: "Katie, I know you miss Bobbye. I know you don't trust me yet. But she's gone, and I'm who's here. I promise to look after you and love you. You can die if you want to, but I hope you won't. Now you decide."

I went in, feeling sad and helpless. The next morning, looking out with trepidation, I saw Katie standing shakily by her water bowl. Water was streaming off her chin.

She improved slowly, getting a little stronger each day. The morning she chased my car I realized that she had recovered. The next night, when a guest appeared, she brought herself forth, in an embarrassing way, on the side of life.

When Katie saw the guest, it was love at first sight —*un coup de foudre.* She yipped and yelped joyously while Weston and I were welcoming him and dealing with his luggage. While Weston served the cocktails, she was shamelessly trying to get all her sixty-five pounds onto his lap. When I tried to drag her off, he said, "Oh, don't worry. I like dogs." With that she nuzzled his armpits and his crotch, French-kissing his lips, his eyes, his ears. It was a disgusting display. I felt I should go in another room, so intimate was this first contact.

She lay at his feet during dinner, her head resting on his shoe. After dinner and conversation over coffee, he excused himself and went to his room. Katie lurked around his door for some time. He evidently got up during the night and let her in; whereupon she must have spent the night in his arms. She emerged looking smug and self-satisfied, but after he left, she walked around the chair where he had sat the night before, looking dejected. "Sorry, Katie. He's gone.

What can I tell you? That's the way it is."

RAIN

VITAL, LIFE-GIVING RAINS HAD not begun. The country was apprehensive and irritable, fearful really. For expats and rich Malawians, this was an inconvenience: water to the low-density areas had been curtailed and watering the lawn with the hose was forbidden. Maki, my gardener after I fired Kennedy, watered the vegetable garden with a watering can. The lawn was bone dry and browned off.

In the high-density areas, water was somewhat more plentiful, thanks to one of our Volunteers who taught the people to petition the mayor for more water. Why should *azungu* and prosperous Malawians fill up their swimming pools and water their roses every day, when poor Malawians (the women, of course), had to carry water on their heads for eight or ten kilometers? Why indeed?

Every day the talk was of rain. One heard that yesterday it had rained in Nsanje, or in Mzuzu, or Mchinji, or at the Lake. There were showers at Nkhata Bay. Thunderclouds were seen over Mulanje. How much rain actually fell in any of these places was never reported. "Just enough to settle the dust," seemed to be the consensus. All of this was pure hearsay, not based on any scientific weather tracking. It was just the talk on the tom-toms. In any case, rain had only fallen once in Lilongwe since my arrival.

I felt that rain would fall soon, or the fields that were planted in corn would dry up and the people would starve. Massive amounts of food aid would be necessary to prevent widespread famine, but donors were fatigued we were told, tired of giving money for seemingly hopeless causes, "pissing down a rat hole" (I think that was Newt Gingrich's eloquent phrase). "Donor fatigue" was an expression that made my heart ache. Of course, the donors were fatigued. So were the people who carried the water and scratched the dry fields for a few grains of corn so their children wouldn't starve before the rains came.

I had been in Malawi for six weeks before I saw a drop of rain. I got accustomed to the fact that it would not rain; routinely left the windows open; hadn't thought of an umbrella (or seen one except the ones Malawian women use for parasols). But on Saturday morning, Oct. 15, the sky was heavy with the possibility of rain. Usually any cloud cover burned off by 8 or 9 o'clock, but on this day, rain was definitely in the air. Around 4—I was at the nursery with Bobbye—I felt a drop or two. An hour later, what we would call a shower began. At 7, I went out on the *khande* with my supper and watched the rain while I ate.

The smell of the rain was intoxicating, a deep, rich, organic smell I remember only in the country at home. Maybe there isn't enough exposed earth in cities to get that damp, sweet scent. Around 7:30, heavy rain began to fall. It wasn't blowing, so I could continue sitting because the *khande* had a deep overhang. The rain came straight down, pelting the tin roof and causing water to collect in the shallow concrete gutters that surround every Malawian house.

I hadn't realized how much I missed rain. In Washington, even though my apartment had a garden, I was seldom aware of rain. Often, I would wake up and realize that rain had fallen during the night, but six stories between the rain and me completely muffled the sound.

When the rain reached a crescendo, I went inside. Then the lights went out. I typed sitting up in bed, operating the computer on batteries and using a flashlight and three candles for illumination. The rain sounded like an all-night rain, like a rain falling over the whole earth. The rainy season, which began in November, promised serious, daily rain for several months, and I anticipated enjoying this pleasure many more times.

LOST ON THE BACK ROADS OF MALAWI

PART OF A SIX-DAY trip to make site visits involved
Bobbye and me in a trip to Nsanje, a small town in the
extreme south, on the Mozambican border. Because
fifteen cases of bubonic plague had been reported
there, the two Peace Corps girls who worked at the
hospital needed reassurance and medicine. Nsanje
was hot. We only intended to stay an hour or so and
then head out for Mulanje via the Thylo (pronounced
Cholo) road. When we pulled out of the hospital
parking lot, we asked a group of Malawians hanging
out at the corner if we were on the road to Thylo; they

assured us that we were. We drove for an hour and a half. Night was falling. The road was full of people walking and bicycling, but we didn't see any cars for long periods. The road was full of "*azungu* traps," shallow concrete dips in the dirt road—some kind of drainage system, probably designed by a Peace Corps Volunteer. Just as I started feeling doubtful about the road, a *mzungu* in a vehicle like ours approached from the opposite direction. I signaled to him to stop and asked, "Is it far to Thylo?" He looked puzzled and said in that disbelieving tone that makes the heart sink, "Thylo? You're on the road to Chikwawa." He said that forty kilometers ahead we would come to the edge of the escarpment. The road to Blantyre would present itself there. Since we were trying to get to Mulanje and not back to Blantyre, we were discouraged; but we pressed on.

I felt fearful, like the children in the fairy tales who were always going deeper into the forest and could not see the breadcrumbs pointing the way. We were probably safer than we would have been in northwest Washington; but something about the darkness, the loneliness of the road, and the fact that no one for miles could speak English, troubled me. Meanwhile, as we went through the villages, the people were still out on the roads—carrying pails of water or bundles of firewood on their heads. I couldn't believe that there was so much life going on in the dark. In Lilongwe, the streets were deserted by 8:30.

Finally, we came to the T in the road at the foot of the escarpment. Here we saw crowds of people. It was like a truck stop back home—people cooking stuff, selling stuff, looking under the hoods of trucks, or just chatting by the side of the road. After turning onto the Blantyre road, Bobbye took the wheel and drove us over the twisting road that led up and then down the escarpment. Upon arriving in Blantyre an hour later, we abandoned any idea of going on to Mulanje and checked into the Mount Sochi Hotel. We ate supper, and then retired to our rooms. I turned out the light at 9:30, but it felt like 1 or 2 in the morning.

THE CHARCOAL SELLERS

BY NOW, THE HOUSEHOLD STAFF had begun to assume that I would bring them something when I returned from trips. The children gathered around and clapped when I drove through the gate. The guards and gardeners stopped what they were doing to greet me with that "Did you bring me something?" look on their faces, unmistakable to anyone who has ever been a parent.

On the last day at the Livingstonia, which was at Salima, right on Lake Malawi, we asked the hotel personnel to send fish sellers around on the morning we left. They came with lots of *chambo* and bigger fish that looked like catfish to me. They stashed them in the back of our pickup where they remained in the heat until we left, around 12:30. By then, the flies were swarming over them. I asked about ice and got uncomprehending looks. The boys on our staff assured me that the fish wouldn't spoil before we got back to Lilongwe. I had already decided to give my share to them, a decision I didn't regret two hours later when we finally got home, and the catch smelled decidedly ripe.

We also stopped to buy charcoal and firewood, which people on the Salima road sell much cheaper than merchants in town. We passed many small roadside sellers, but the drivers already had a place in mind—probably run by a brother-in-law of one of them. As we pulled up beside the designated place, I longed for my camera. The charcoal operation looked like a family ran it. Forty or fifty people crowded around our caravan of three vans and the truck. The drivers got out to negotiate a good price—a volume discount, I guess. I stayed in the truck, shaking hands and talking through the window to the children who stood four-deep around the truck, staring at my *mzungu* hair and skin. When I spoke to them in *Chichewa*, they all tittered. I must have been really bad.

The price agreed upon, the charcoal sellers starting loading the sacks and the bundles into the vans and trucks, on top of the fish and our *kitundu*. I hoped my suitcase would smell of charcoal and eucalyptus instead of spoiling fish.

When Steven, our driver, got back in, I asked him the size and price of the bags of charcoal. When he told me, my heart sank. The bags of charcoal weighing about sixty pounds, sold for fifteen *kwacha* each or roughly one dollar in US currency since the devaluation. God knows how much wood the people must have burned to reduce it to sixty pounds of briquettes; but in a country where deforestation was the number one environmental problem, these people were selling their future and the future of their children for a criminally small amount of money because they couldn't do anything else. Conservation was then a *mzungu* abstraction. Who could think of "conservation" when the family needed *nsima* to get through another day?

I wondered why all the donor agencies and research teams weren't working on alternate sources of fuel. Without that, I felt that Malawi would look like Haiti in another ten years, maybe less. If I had been president of the country I would have made AIDS and alternate fuel sources my two top priorities. Right after that, I would have gone for the infant mortality rate—one of the highest in the world—and the female literacy rate—one of the lowest in the world.

I didn't know whether Muluzi would be able to govern this country so that it would look more like Botswana or Zimbabwe and less like Zaire or Angola. The newspapers criticized him and his cabinet for taking trips to Europe and the States and for driving Mercedes-Benzes. His predecessor—His Excellency Hastings Banda—had eleven sumptuous palaces, so I guess Muluzi's extravagances represented an improvement.

If I had been Muluzi, I would have called in the Cabinet and said something like, "O.K., Fellas, I want the IMR down below seventy-five before anyone takes another trip to Paris or New York. Get it under fifty, and we'll talk Mercedes. In the meantime, turn in your Merc. Here are the keys to a motorcycle. If the Infant Mortality Rate is still above two hundred in six months, you will turn in your motorcycle keys and receive a bicycle or bus fare to and from your home. I'm serious. Now get the hell out of here and go to work."

GIVING UP CONTROL

PEACE CORPS VOLUNTEERS HAD a unique interpretation of hospitality. It could be simply stated: if there was free food, they were going to be there. Vyrle and I decided to take the Volunteers out to dinner when we were passing through Blantyre, so I counted them and added four more (Vyrle, his wife Dolly, their son Josh and me). I made reservations for twelve at the nicest restaurant in Blantyre—L'Hostaria, an Italian oasis in that part of Africa. When we arrived at the restaurant, it became obvious that we had many more than twelve in our party. The proprietor extended the table to accommodate sixteen guests, and even with that, we had to squeeze in three or four more. I was mildly annoyed because I had handled the arrangements and thought everything was under control, but *no*. One Volunteer had heard about the dinner and had come up from Thylo, another one blew in from Chikwawa, a third included his girl friend who was passing through town. The others crawled out from somewhere. Vyrlc was nonplussed, as he was about everything; but I was astounded that people would come without an invitation and annoyed that what I thought was handled wasn't handled at all.

The week preceding the dinner, I had been hostess for a sit-down dinner for what I assumed would be ten-twelve people. The occasion was an in-service training day for the Parks and Wildlife Volunteers, who were my responsibility. I had thought it would be nice if they and their Malawian counterparts had dinner at my house instead of at a restaurant. I asked Weston to set sixteen places, just in case, and seventeen showed up! Vyrle brought Dolly and Josh, which surprised me because I had issued only the most perfunctory of invitations—as in "I wouldn't imagine that Dolly and Josh would want to come, but if they do..." One brought a buddy who was tramping around the world and just happened to be in Malawi. So the count reached fifteen, but this presented no problem; I'd set up for sixteen. Things went off the rails when the Volunteers brought in their driver and installed him. When Mr. Mphande, the Parks boss, saw him, he sent for his driver as well, which made one more person than I could accommodate. Weston was outraged and said that drivers did not eat at table; the cook was supposed to give them a Fanta and any leftovers after the meal. I had a little problem with that practice, but since the drivers had spun my dinner party out of control—it really wasn't their fault; they seemed acutely uncomfortable—I was more than a little annoyed because the situation felt like an abuse of hospitality.

I could already see that trying to maintain any control over events like these was an invitation to frustration. After two of these events, I decided that Volunteers weren't necessarily rude and poorly brought up. Evidently, the "one-come-all-come" mentality was part of the Peace Corps culture. Another interesting thing was that they rarely said "thank you," another astonishment. Oddly enough, I experienced more astonishments adjusting to Peace Corps culture than I did adjusting to the Malawian one. Peace Corps understanding about food, parties, and hospitality in general would be a good training for me. According to the Enneagram, I was Number 2 which indicated that I loved to give generously and often, but I also liked to control the way I gave, and I required acknowledgment, sometimes massive acknowledgment, to feel good after my giving. Life was just one opportunity for growth after another!

LIVINGSTONIA GETAWAY

IN UNDER AN HOUR, I could drive from my office in Lilongwe to the Livingstonia Beach Hotel, an old establishment left over from colonial days, situated on the southern shore of Lake Malawi. I went as often as I could to get away from the pressures of work. It was another world. Upon driving through the gate, a Malawian in a spiffy safari suit would do the little stamp and salute left behind by the British. There was always a register to be signed. One of the blanks on the form asked for citizenship, vehicle tag number, and colour. That seemed a bit regressive to me, but the Livingstonia Beach was like that, a little remnant of the nineteenth century. Someone told me later that the blank asking for *colour* indicated the color of the automobile.

Usually my visits to the Livingstonia were pleasant interludes I used to change the pace, get a little rest, and catch up on my reading and writing. However, this particular visit was something of a personal emergency, an attack of devastating fatigue brought on by three weeks of high intensity on the job. At this point, The Livingstonia Beach Hotel would serve as my personal retreat house.

The place looks like any upscale resort in any tropical place—the Caribbean, for example. An outdoor bar, a broad terrace for meals, white cottages around the pool, lots of tropical vegetation— bougainvillea, coconut and Queen palms, hibiscus, gardenia. The hotel itself was surrounded by deep, blue-green lawns, trimmed daily by Malawian men in uniforms with shorts. They kept the grass impeccably trimmed with scissors.

My favorite feature was the string of little *rondavelles*—round stucco huts with thatched roofs right on the beach. I always requested the one farthest from the club. Beyond it was a small village, complete with Malawians out tending their nets, cooking, washing clothes, and singing. In the distance, I could hear tom-toms. I once had the idea that the Livingstonia paid those folks to live there and act like local people for the atmospheric quality they would provide to the clientele.

I went to my *rondavelle* immediately after checking in. I did not want to see anyone or talk to anyone, or have any intense cultural exchanges. I only wanted to fall asleep with my clothes on, which I promptly did.

When I awoke, it was dark, totally dark as only a tropical place can be. I was too tired to go to supper. I didn't want to order food because I was too exhausted to decide what I wanted or pick up the phone to order anything. I went back to sleep around 8 p.m. and was awakened around first light by the villagers next door.

All that day I drowsed under a beach umbrella or napped in my room. I knew in the back of my mind that I could be called at any moment to handle a crisis. I knew I could spring up if that happened, but I devoutly hoped it wouldn't. It was the nature of my job that I was hardly ever alone and never anonymous. Even in villages with which I wasn't familiar, people would say, "Ah, La Directrice." I wasn't anonymous at the LBH, but the staff was extremely discreet.

Around suppertime, the hotel manager, a nice Malawian lady named Gladys, came to the umbrella and asked if she could speak to me. She said she was worried because she hadn't seen me since my arrival and wondered if I needed anything. Supper was ready, chicken with rice, she said. When I told her I was too tired to dress and come up, she told me that a tray would arrive in thirty minutes and asked if I wanted a gin-tonic or a scotch-soda. I said a gin would be much appreciated. When it came, I drank it off like medicine before my dinner arrived.

All this gentle caretaking was balm to my spirit. After my dinner, I showered and went back to bed, read a page or two, and then fell back into a profound sleep.

When I awoke it was almost first light of Sunday morning, the last day of my little vacation. I went down to the beach and sat on the sand, listening to the waves and waiting for the sun to come up. The moon and the Morning Star were still visible. Gradually the clouds turned salmon and pink, like cotton candy with a lot of orange in the mix. The sun was a long time rising above the bank of clouds that stretched like a thick ribbon along the horizon. Finally, it broke through.

Impelled by I don't know what primitive urge, I stood up, stepped out of my shorts and shirt, and walked out into the water. When the water reached shoulder height, I lay back and submerged my head and face. Then I stood up and walked back to shore, surprised by my sudden elemental baptismal urge.

The lake is ancient, formed during the dinosaur age when massive upheavals in the earth's crust created the entire Rift Valley, a slash in the earth from the Red Sea to southernmost east Africa. Lake Malawi is 350 miles long (Washington to North Carolina.) Much of Malawi's history has taken place on the shores of this vast inland sea—the coming of the Arabs, the commerce of the slave traders, the discoveries of Dr. Livingstone, the arrival of the Missionaries, the fall of the indigenous culture, and colonization by the British.

So who knows what mysterious forces were at work there, forces that caused unsuspecting *azungu* to throw off their clothes and plunge into its warm, fresh waters?

When I got out, I felt repaired, released, and ready to take up my load again. I had breakfast under the umbrella, settled my bill, and said goodbye to Gladys. When I drove through the gate, a different Malawian stamped and saluted. As I was pulling away, he said, "Come back soon, Madam."

The people who went to the Livingstonia were mostly but not all white. Some well-to-do Malawians went there, but mostly the clientele was American and European. The plump, pink men— Germans, Dutch, and Brits—were usually accompanied by gorgeous, long-legged, blonde girls, who were taller, thinner, and younger. I have seen several "mixed couples," usually really handsome black men with white women. In the *rondavelle* next to mine a spectacularly well-muscled black guy and a fair-haired white girl were installed. He was too big to be a Malawian, and she was too long of limb to be an American or a Brit. When I passed them on the beach, I heard them speaking French. Racially mixed couples didn't seem to incite the kind of curiosity and covert (sometimes overt) hostility they did at that time in the States.

When night fell, the management sent round some candles and informed the patrons that they wouldn't be turning on the lights because the electricity had been off all day and was still off. When it was time for dinner, I set off, candle in hand. The flame almost went out several times, which was a little scary because the night was so dark. I wasn't sure where I was putting my feet. I tried not to think about black *mambas*.

The experience of dining by candlelight in the darkened restaurant was exotic, but the menu was the usual international fare with a few African dishes thrown in. Once back at the *rondavelle*, there wasn't enough light to read by, so I lay listening to the waves lapping the beach until I drifted off to sleep. When I woke up at first light, around 4 o'clock, I went out to the beach. I sat for what seemed half an hour or so, watching the stars fade and the sky turn soft shades of pink. After a lot of buildup, the sun jumped up over the horizon, a sunrise that happened in the blink of an eye. I wish I could remember Kipling's poem that says, "The dawn came up like thunder..." Something about "Looking eastward to the bay." After the sunrise, I read a bit of Graham Greene's autobiography, *A Sort of Life*—another Brit writing about his experience in the colonies. I planned to reread all those guys, including Hemingway's chronicles about Africa, plus Isak Dinesen, Beryl Markham, and all that lot.

VICTORIA FALLS

I WENT TO ZIMBABWE FOR a few days one early October. I was all set to go to Ethiopia with Dana, a Volunteer who was returning to the States after her Close of Service via Addis Ababa and other exotic places. Her host family mother had recently been appointed Ambassador to Ethiopia from Malawi. Unfortunately, we were not able to arrange visas, so we went to Zimbabwe instead. Harare, a one-hour flight from Lilongwe, 150 US dollars, was another world. A regular city of over a million, it has tall buildings, shops, cinemas, jazz, and cappuccino—all the civilized delights so notably absent in Malawi. I once heard a woman say that she didn't want to go to any country where you had to take your own toilet tissue and where they didn't know who Estee Lauder was. In Harare, certain people in certain shops have heard of

Estee Lauder, and they have toilet paper handled as well.

After Dana left to climb Mt. Kilimanjaro, I went up to Victoria Falls by myself. I booked a comfortable but ordinary hotel within walking distance of the falls and stayed there three days. I arrived in the late afternoon, and set out for the falls the next morning.

It was impossible to miss the falls. I walked into the little town, whose only reason for being was to service the tourist trade—the safari tours at the high end of the scale, and the overlanders and backpackers at the other. I passed the string of outfitters shops and places to arrange for white water rafting and bungee jumping off the bridge. Turning left at the fast food place (I forget which one), following the sound of roaring water, and walking toward the clouds of spray that looked like smoke from a distance got me to the park in fifteen minutes.

After the usual tourist thing—buy the ticket, have your hand stamped, get the map —I headed up the path leading to "Devil's Cataract." Everyone said the Zambezi River was too low for the falls to be dramatic, but I was simply knocked out. The word "awesome," in spite of its recent debasement, was the only one that worked.

After I stared at the falls for a few moments, I knew I didn't want to see them in the presence of other tourists—mostly Americans and Europeans wearing neatly creased safari clothes straight out of the box, and hats, like pith helmets, that only hotel doormen wore. They would come up the path, usually with a guide, and look, usually briefly, at the falls. Soon they would take pictures of each other with the falls in the background, get the guide to take their pictures altogether, then go away. Been there; done that; where's the T-shirt?

Meanwhile, the sound of the "African Thunder,"

as the indigenous people called the falls, was in competition with the constant buzz of low-flying airplanes carrying more tourists to see the sight from above. I decided to walk the path for a bit and get a general sense of the falls, then figure out a way to see them by myself.

When I left, I asked the gatekeeper what time the park opened and what time people started to come. He said it opened at 6 a.m., but people didn't come until later in the morning. They closed at 6 p.m., but usually the park was nearly empty by 4:30 or 5 p.m. Ah ha!

I walked back the long way, past the famous old Victoria Falls Hotel, familiar to anyone who reads glossy travel or food magazines. I had considered staying there, but $200 a night for a single brought me to my senses. I also considered the possibility of having lunch on the veranda, until I saw the place. A luxurious, sprawling, white, colonial-style watering hole set deep in a broad expanse of emerald green lawn, in a country that often doesn't have enough rain to keep people alive. It smelled of money, boredom, and death. I passed an American couple, looking like American tourists tend to look, arguing peevishly about whether to lunch at the hotel or at the newly opened Elephant Hills, for the novelty. I kept walking.

Early the next morning I set out again. The gatekeeper told me I was only the third person to enter. It crossed my mind that the other two were homicidal maniacs now loose in a totally unattended expanse of bush. I bought the ticket and went in.

I returned to the spot at which I had started the day before and communed a bit with the spirit of Dr. Livingstone near his statue. He looked like many eminent nineteenth and early twentieth century men —Freud, Albert Schweitzer, Mark Twain, even Faulkner. The base of the statue read: Dr. David

Livingstone—Explorer, Missionary, Scientist, Humanitarian. Not bad for one lifetime. I presume.

After a bit, I stood facing the falls, hearing the roar without the airplane accompaniment, feeling the mist on my face. I watched the massive volume of water hurl itself over the cliff and fall straight down into the boiling pool below. I watched individual drops, fall one at a time, all the way down. I lost track of time. I couldn't break my gaze. I was, briefly, one with the falls.

As the sun rose higher, turning the sky all shades of pink, I left and walked the trail again, going farther than I had the day before and stopping at each vantage point.

The most memorable part of this trek was the rainforest. Waist-high, brown grass that reminded me of Hemingway novels bordered the trail and followed the length of the falls on the Zimbabwe side. It was the kind of grass that suggests a lion could jump out at any moment. The days I was there, it was hot and dusty—the real Africa. At one point, the trail led into a thick, jungled grove of trees, a contrast from the dry grass and scrubby bushes. The temperature dropped perceptibly, and the spray from the falls fell like a light rain. Suddenly, I realized that this little patch was a rain forest—complete with lush trees, twisted vines and ground cover, even exotic, jungle-like birds and a baboon or two. I couldn't believe it. It was like stepping into another country. I walked for what seemed like a city block before the trail led out of the forest and back into the bush, the heat, the dust, the drought.

I wished someone had been there to explain a little bit about this phenomenon. I assumed that the chasm narrowed at this point so that the spume from the falls on the opposite side reached across and kept that little patch moist all the time, creating rainforest conditions. Sound good?

ON ZOMBA
MOUNTAIN

ZOMBA, THE OLD COLONIAL CAPITAL, was one of the four
principal towns in Malawi, along with Blantyre
(named for the home in Scotland of Dr. Livingston),
Lilongwe, and Mzuzu. It was about an hour's drive
from Blantyre, on a road that went over the
escarpment. Zomba itself was a charming little town.
Because of the elevation, it was cooler than most other
places and could get quite cold at night. The town was
at the foot of Zomba Mountain. A thirty-minute drive
on a steep road up the mountain took us to the
Plateau, where the American Embassy maintained a
cottage. The cottage was actually built by a Peace
Corps Volunteer, but when the Peace Corps was asked
to leave in the late seventies, the Embassy took it over

and refused to give it back. One had to reserve it and pay $60 a night to stay there (little enough, I suppose, but it was mildly galling to think that we *could* have been staying there free whenever we liked.) The Embassy had installed a flagpole, upon which, I assume, the Stars and Stripes were run up when the Ambassador was in residence. Really! I planned to go there often and bring guests. Maybe I'd fly a flag that said "Carpe Diem" or "Live Juicy" whenever I visited.

After dropping in on the training in the village, Bobbye and I reached the cottage around 4 in the afternoon. Within minutes of our arrival, a gang of six or eight black children arrived with pans of berries—strawberries, blackberries, and both red and yellow raspberries. They also had fresh rhubarb. Next time I went, I told myself I'd make strawberry and rhubarb pie. The climate up there was conducive to the cultivation of exceptional fruits and vegetables. I had seen strawberries and tomatoes in the shops of Lilongwe and Blantyre that were billed as "Zomba berries" or "tomatoes from Zomba."

At the cottage, we stayed outdoors almost all the time. One morning we ate breakfast on the porch, and I put a table out on the lawn and wrote there almost all morning. That night we walked to the Ku Chawe to have a gin and tonic and watch the sun go down. The cloud cover was too dense to see much more than a few rose-colored streaks behind the mountain, and shortly after six, it began to rain. The rain fell so gently at first that we didn't move, and when it started coming down more generously, we moved to a table with a large umbrella. After a bit, we decided to walk home in the rain. On the way back to the cottage, I smelled the intense smell of pine rosin (resin), a scent I remember from the piney woods of western Louisiana and eastern Texas. It also reminded me of the rosin that string players use on their bows for better traction with the strings.

The evening was cool, cooler than usual because of the rain. When we neared the cottage, we could see the lights from the windows and smell wood smoke from the chimney. Dennis had made a large fire for us. We let him leave and prepared our own supper, which we ate on trays in front of the fire. We had no real groceries. We had brought wine and fresh vegetables, and we had lots of berries, but that was about it. No olive oil, no seasonings, no bread, no rice —none of the usual staples. I broiled some tiny eggplants and red peppers while Bobbye cooked tomatoes, onions, and carrots in a pan. We poured the vegetable sauce over the grilled eggplants and peppers and baked the lot. That, with a glass or two of South African cabernet, was our supper. We topped it off with fresh blackberries and milk left over from breakfast.

I don't know when I've tasted anything so wonderful. How could this be? No basil, no rosemary, no cheese, no pasta—just vegetables and then fruit for dessert? All the vegetables had come from my garden, and the berries had been picked that morning. Maybe it was that everything was fresh; maybe it was that the mountain air had made us hungry, but the meal was so delicious that I wondered where we had conceived the idea that we had to have all the seasonings, cheese, and pasta.

The cottage grounds were informally landscaped, but the path leading to the house was lined on both sides with rosebushes. Dennis and Susan, the Malawian couple who lived on the place and did the cooking and cleaning, had put fresh roses in every room. After a solid nine hours of profound sleep, I sat on the *khande*, staring up at the mountain, drinking coffee and eating raspberries and gingerbread. All that and roses on the table was almost more than I could bear.

The air on Zomba Mountain was always soft and mild, sometimes misty. Many of the trees were coniferous, so the smell of pine and cedar was always in the air. Bobbye and I went for an hour-long walk down a red dirt road to a lake that had been stocked with trout. Beyond the lake, we followed a narrow path alongside a stream. As the path went gently upward, the vegetation became thicker. I kept hoping to see a monkey and not a Green Mamba, a deadly snake whose bite reputedly kills in three steps—you step near it and it bites, you take the second step, and on the third step you fall dead. I didn't see a monkey or a snake, only dense forest and the stream fringed with fern and full of big boulders. I identified the place as one of the world's great picnic spots. Toward the end of the walk, as the trail led higher, we came upon a series of waterfalls that fed a shallow pool, perfect for wading except that the water was probably cold. The trail came out near the Ku Chawe Inn, famous as a great place to stay or just to have a drink and watch the sunset. Each room had its own garden and fireplace. It wasn't one of the three-star inns of Africa, but the food was pleasant enough.

Just beyond the Ku Chawe, we saw a group of boys in blue shirts and khaki pants. I found out that they were schoolboys. Kids didn't go to school on Saturday, but these guys were with their teacher on a nature hike. I also saw some older boys absorbed in a vigorous game of soccer in the road, using what looked like balled-up plastic trash bags tied with cord. When they saw us, they stopped abruptly, apologized, and moved to the side of the road.

We planned to move our training site from Blantyre to Zomba, where the facility was nicer, the price cheaper, and the town filled with middle-class Malawians—civil servants and college folks. We had home stay visits for our Volunteers. The families in Blantyre were entirely too rich for our purposes. Zomba families would probably be more representative although they were certainly not villagers. I loved Zomba and looked forward to spending time there.

TROUBLE IN
PARADISE

UPON MY RETURN FROM A six weeks' sojourn in the States, I learned that my yard had been broken into by a group of men attempting to steal the generator, a useless luxury provided by the Peace Corps for my use during power outages. I say useless because although the power failed regularly, it never stayed off for longer than an hour or two. The generator was noisy and belched noxious fumes, and I hadn't turned it on once since it had been installed.

Nevertheless, it represented a considerable sum of money. The intruders had cut the wire fence surrounding the house and garden and moved the generator out into the street when one of the guards woke up and sounded the alarm. The men ran away, the police came, Weston woke up and took charge, the whole neighborhood was aroused by this time, and Paul (our admin officer) and Osborne (our General Services Officer) came too.

The story got muddier when the night guard, Flatware, told the police that he recognized Kennedy, the gardener, as one of the men. By the time I returned home, Paul had fired Kennedy, who was awaiting trial, and installed Anton, an inexperienced gardener he was employing out of charity to help his regular gardener.

Meanwhile, Kennedy had accused Weston of petty thievery and conspiring to steal a bicycle from the Peace Corps warehouse. The day guard also said that Weston had allowed some of his relatives onto the compound while I was away. (He lived on the compound, but PC regulation forbade him to allow guests to drive a car through the gates without my permission).

All this made me sick at heart but was part and parcel of life in the Third World. I asked Kennedy to come to the office so I could find out what happened, according to his version of it. He told this Kafkaesque tale of being awakened in the middle of the night by armed police, handcuffed, taken to the police station, beaten and kicked without any explanation of what he was accused of or who had accused him. He languished in jail for ten days before his brother-in-law paid his bail and he was released to await trial. Meanwhile, Flatware identified him as the man he had seen the night of the break-in.

Kennedy was freed but could not get a job. He said his children were starving; they weren't going to school because he couldn't pay their school fees, etc.

I sent for Flatware, and Ledson and Osborne translated my questions to him regarding the incident. Nothing he said made sense or hung together logically. It was pretty clear to me that Kennedy was asleep in his bed when the whole thing happened. Why would Flatware lie? Was he in on the deal (guards often were). What was Weston's connection, if any, with all of this? What could I do?

The Peace Corps didn't want me to rehire Kennedy until it was clear that he didn't have anything to do with the theft of PC property. I hired another gardener that I liked. Besides, I had loaned Kennedy 1,500 *kwacha* (about $100) to buy a sewing machine so he could generate extra income, so I felt as though I'd done plenty.

I didn't press the matter of Weston's possible involvement. I depended on him so much and trusted him so thoroughly that I just didn't want to face up to questioning him and letting him confront his accusers. Meanwhile, Kennedy, clearly a victim of human rights violations, continued to suffer.

I thought about getting rid of the whole passel of them and doing the house and yard work myself; but that was an impossibility. One needed, I was told, to have men on the place to protect against robbery and worse. Malawians didn't understand the idea of a woman living alone, and it was best not to go against the received wisdom of the office staff.

This was the dark side of coming home to a clean house, a well-tended garden, and a hot meal.

KITUNDU AND NJINGA

TWO VITAL WORDS IN *Chichewa*, the language of southern Malawi, were *kitundu* and *njinga*. Without *njinga* or bicycles, *kitundu* or "stuff" cannot be easily moved. Because *njinga* were expensive and few could afford them, people learned to use their bodies as a means of transporting their *kitundu* wherever it needed to go. Seeing people carrying huge loads was a common sight on the roads and along the footpaths through the bush.

Men and women carried sheets of tin, logs of firewood, sacks of grain, boxes and parcels of all sizes. I once saw a man with enough straw on his head to thatch the roof of his hut. Portable sewing machines on the heads of men was a familiar sight in both villages and towns as itinerant tailors bore their machines through the neighborhoods, accompanied by small boys with folded squares of brightly colored fabric stacked on their heads. When they heard the cry "Hey, Tailor, over here!" they went to the person who wanted work done.

Often the client selected the fabric he wanted on the spot, and the tailor cut, sewed, and finished the garment that same day. For more intricate designs and higher quality fabrics, such as the beautiful and intricate wax patterns and refined batiks, the client would normally visit a shop in town.

While the men seemed to be the bearers of the largest loads, the women and girls also had to carry *kitundu*. A baby was not *kitundu*, but the female bearers of *kitundu* had to transport their smallest child along with everything else. The concept of babysitters, daycare, preschool, and all the other institutions that ease the burdens of motherhood in industrial societies were mostly not available to African women. So from a baby's earliest days, as soon as it was strong enough to hold up its head, until the age of two, sometimes three, they were carried about on their mothers' backs. Meanwhile, the women went on with their lives quite naturally, pulling water, pounding meal, cooking, washing, shopping, working in the fields, and carrying things. One saw women with buckets of water on their heads, huge bundles of clothes, baskets of bread, pans of fish or fruit, and large bags of maize flour. The baby behind was usually asleep, and if he wasn't, he made no fuss.

The African women and girls I saw every day were remarkably sure-footed and poised, almost casual in their movements. I have seen women jump across a ditch with a bucket of water on her head and a baby on her back, never sloshing a drop or jolting the child. They were as skilled as circus performers. I marveled at their grace and sense of balance and their strength. I watched a woman of about my size, pulling water from a well nearby. Her biceps bulged with the effort. She rested a moment, preparing to lift the bucket onto her head. I asked her if she thought I would be able to carry it on my head. "No, Ma'am," she said, "It would snap your neck." She smiled as she coiled the piece of twisted fabric she would set on her head as a cradle to keep the pail from slipping. "African women are strong," she said, starting down the path with long, confident strides. "We have to be. And we start young."

And indeed they did. Small girls begin carrying their brothers and sisters on their backs when they were not much bigger than the child. One day, I saw Weston's little girl, Helen, walking up the driveway with a teddy bear tied on her back and a shoebox balanced on her head. She was four at the time and already in training to bear her burdens gracefully.

As babies get bigger and heavier, they begin to try to direct their mother's activities. I saw one trying to reach around and unbutton his mother's blouse and another carrying her mother's purse and fiddling with the clasp. Sometimes they bucked a little, as if to say, "Come on, giddy-up." The young ones made only gentle suggestions; these children were never impatient or pushy.

The most remarkable thing to me was the way in which a woman placed a child on her own back without assistance. She did it with one hand by grasping the baby by its upper arm, bending slightly, then slinging it up onto her back. Then she folded a long piece of cotton cloth to make a *tchinge*, slung it up, grabbed both ends and tied them in one deft motion. When the baby was properly loaded, she went forward on her ceaseless round of tasks.

The mothers never carried diaper bags, baby

bottles, tissues, baby wipes, pacifiers, toys, or any of the other paraphernalia so necessary for western children. African babies were either at the breast or on the back. When I thought of the hundreds of dollars Americans spend on strollers, baby carriages, and all the rest of it, I wondered which children were the happiest. As part of the Bigification of Everything in America, a child's stroller now takes up most of the sidewalk, and yet the pampered little riders are often fretful and demanding. In contrast, Malawian babies seldom cried unless they were sick or in pain. They were by nature sweet, patient, and contented. Maybe they didn't demand attention because they got so much "body time" with their mothers, who were always busy but never hurried and never far away. For at least two years the child lived as an extension of its mother's body, was lovingly cared for, and also nurtured by other women in the family and the community as their own. A stroller as big as an SUV seems little compensation for that.

Obviously, the babies liked riding on their mother's back. I sometimes wondered what it would be like to have a child on my back as I went through the day's work. One day, Maki the garden boy, as these workers were called, brought his tiny wife Elizabeth, only a few weeks out of childbed, to show me their newborn. The baby was named Harrison, or so I thought. I later discovered that his name was Allison. Many Malawians, like the Chinese, have trouble with the letter L, which sometimes comes out as an R. Allison had been sleeping soundly when they arrived; but when he started stirring, I asked to hold him. Elizabeth handed him over, and he continued his nap, undisturbed. As the visit was winding down, she took the *tchinge* he was wrapped in and began to fold it to make the baby's sling so she could put him on her back. On an impulse, I asked if she would put him on my back for a few minutes before they left. She seemed startled, but she and Maki motioned for me to bend over. They placed the infant a little below my shoulder blades, and Elizabeth wrapped the sling around him, brought the corners around to the front and tied them tightly around my ribcage. The baby struggled while we fussed with the *tchinge*, but once he was firmly fastened on, he snuggled down and went back to sleep. Baby Onboard.

He fit comfortably on my back, a satisfying little load. Maki, Elizabeth, and I walked around the garden; and when they saw that I wasn't ready to give the baby up, we strolled up the road in front of my house. Passersby looked at us curiously, as if the sight of a *mzungu* with a black child on her back was extraordinary. I guess it was. When they left, Elizabeth whispered something to Maki in *Chichewa*, which he translated as, "Amayi said, 'Thank you for touching our baby.'"

Transporting *kitundu* and kids was one thing, but strong as Malawians were and as accustomed from childhood to carrying heavy loads as they were, there were limits to the amount of *kitundu* they could carry. The Malawians profited in the colonial period when the British introduced the bicycle into the territory. They named the contraption *njinga* in imitation of the sound of the bell. For them the *njinga* was not a recreational vehicle or a toy but a means of transporting themselves and their *kitundu* as well.

Men rode with large, specially adapted baskets of goods strapped on behind. These wire or willow baskets, as much as three or four feet wide, were used to carry chickens or rabbits. Although Malawians rode when the load was light enough, they used the bicycle most often as we would use a luggage cart. They pushed the thing along loaded with pieces of lumber, goat carcasses, sacks of charcoal, or loads of firewood.

For transporting the latter, they often affixed a wooden rack to the back of the bike, which allowed them to stack the logs up even higher than their heads. I once saw a man riding a bike with a sofa strapped on the back. Fortunately there were few cars on that road because he took up as much room as a truck.

One day I received a visit from a young American who told me he was riding from Cape-to-Cairo for "Pedals for Progress," an organization whose mission was to collect used and discarded bicycles for distribution in developing countries When my apartment building back in Washington, DC, decreed that residents must claim and tag their bikes in the bike room by a certain date or they would be given to charity, "Pedals for Progress" made a haul. I cannot imagine an African moving away and abandoning a bicycle. I remembered that in Africa used clothing markets were called "Dead Men's Markets" because Africans couldn't understand why wearable clothes were being put up for sale unless the owner had died.

Curiously, as valuable as bicycles were in Africa, women in Malawi did not ride them. I saw Weston's big girl Monica riding his bike around the garden, but she never took it onto the street. I suspect it was the attachment to modesty that Malawians possessed. Women and girls couldn't show their legs or wear pants, which excluded a lot of activities we take for granted. During my time in Africa, "Pedals for Progress" hadn't been extended to women yet.

THE NEW
HEDONISM,
AFRICAN STYLE

IN AFRICA, FREQUENT AND REGULAR visits to beauty
salons were new experiences for me. I only went to
"beauty parlors," as they were called in the South, to
get my hair cut a couple of weeks after it really needed
it. Everything else took too long or offended my
puritanical streak—I'm supposed to be an intellectual,
etc., etc., and one could save a whole village in Africa
for what some women spent on their nails, etc. etc.;
there were more important things to do, blah, blah.

I don't know quite what changed all that—
working fourteen hours a day, feeling as though the

African sun and air were beating me up, wanting someone to pamper me. In any case, I started having my nails done, and since I was there, I had my legs waxed, then I decided that a facial every now and again would be nice, and finally I had a South African-trained French woman who did massages, aromatherapy, luxurious pedicures, and foot massage. Where would it end? I guess it was all part of living like a princess (and not having had a date in ten months). *C'est l'Afrique, quoi.* And it was cheap, incredibly cheap by American standards.

Malawian beauty salons were almost all run by Indians, with Malawian girls doing most of the work. African women came in occasionally, but the clientele was largely Indian. The young Indian women were often startlingly beautiful and well cared for. Even the teen-agers came in for regular facials on Saturday. They joked in *Chichewa* with the salon attendants since they were all fluent in the local language, most of them having been born in Malawi.

Many of the older women still retained vestiges of great beauty. Most were quite heavy, some even grossly fat by our standards. They seemed to like themselves that way. They didn't talk about their weight, their diets, their exercise programs in the obsessive way American women do. They just lolled around, looking languid and faintly bored, having the dry skin rubbed off their heels and elbows, having even more holes pierced in their ears—the better to wear the fantastic gold jewelry they all seemed to have.

When I discovered the French woman from Mauritius—Isle Maurice—I stopped going to the Indian shop. The Malawian girls had begun to get on my nerves, asking me how many servants I had (a sore point), if I had a boyfriend (another touchy point), when I was going back to the States, and would I take them with me?

Appointments in those shops were difficult because time meant nothing. If a person showed up at the appointed time, she was often told that the hairdresser hadn't come in yet (no transport) or that the water was off, or the manicurist had to go to a funeral in Blantyre, etc. Another annoyance was the pack of stray Malawian girls sitting around, reading the European or South African fashion magazines and giggling with the workers. All in all, the atmosphere was not restful. They also scrutinized white people closely, fascinated by their hair, their skin, their clothes. They talked among themselves, gossiping and laughing. The word "*mzungu*" kept cropping up, leading me to believe that they were having a joke at my expense.

The world of women in beauty salons was a subculture. My Malawi experience called to mind my trip to the Turkish bath in Istanbul after five weeks in the outback of the former Soviet Union, Siberia, and the "Stans." Exhausted from traveling in countries that totally did not work, toxic from pollution, greasy, starchy food, and rotgut vodka (the only comfort at the end of those endless days), and strung out from too much danger (nine flights on Aeroflot, twenty hours on a train through three war zones), I experienced Turkey as a rebirth—fresh linens, hot water, and *café au lait*.

At the Turkish bath, I was the only outsider. The Turkish women sat around completely nude, sipping intense coffee in tiny cups. Almost all were fat, with sagging breasts. Many had unsubtle scars on their bellies—cesareans or something of the sort, I guessed. The sisterhood of surgery. They seemed completely at ease, with their bodies and with each other, laughing, gossiping, and teasing.

The girl who came to splash a bucket of water on

me every few minutes finally motioned to me to take my turn on the heated marble dome, the central feature of this bath for three hundred years. With big sponges and brushes she scrubbed and soaped and splashed one side, then the other. She asked, without words, if I wanted my feet done, my hair. I signaled, "Everything." In the two hours or so that I was there, she managed to convey, without spoken language, that she was unhappy, that she had three kids and a husband who drank, spent the money she made on other women, and beat her regularly. I wasn't sure what the appropriate tip was, but when she mimed surprise and displeasure at what I had given her, I gave her some more. As I was getting dressed, I saw her showing the other women the money, evidently gloating over her good fortune in having a client too stupid to know better and too tired to care.

In spite of this minor irritation, I returned to the hotel in an altered state, went to bed on the clean sheets, slept for eighteen hours, and woke up feeling purified and more or less returned to myself. And all for less than the price of a good haircut in Washington or New York.

SIMPLE
PLEASURES

ONE THURSDAY BEFORE CHRISTMAS, I experienced a lull in the pace of life in Africa, and Sabina (our Program Assistant for Programming and Training) decided to take time off to go shopping. Inside of twenty-five minutes we had selected two desks, two chairs, two "credenzas" (what a pretentious word for a Formica-covered Parson's table), and several roll-around file boxes). We needed all this equipment for the Programming and Training Empire we were building together.

Then we decided to really go shopping. We went to *MACOHA* (Malawi Council for the Handicapped—in Malawi every institution has an acronym), where people with polio, i.e., any disability, made tie-dyed fabrics, African shirts and dresses, and a variety of other crafts.

I bought an African dress—a modified *bou-bou*. Malawian women were much too modest (or much too suppressed) to wear a real West African *bou-bou*, in which one felt, and probably was, *complètement exposé* most of the time. I wanted a dress, which skimmed the body, which did not necessitate any underwear, and which would not scandalize the servants. I bought a beautiful purple and white one with lots of embroidery on the yoke and hem.

When I arrived at home, I learned that Weston, who had been feeling poorly for several days, had given up and wasn't preparing dinner. I felt a momentary panic until I reminded myself that up until the three months I had been in Malawi I had prepared my own dinner nearly every night of my adult life.

I bathed, put on my African dress, and made an omelet with Tex Mex chili beans, fresh cilantro (Sabina and I went to the Chinese shop on our jaunt), and cheddar cheese. These ingredients, along with fresh sliced tomatoes from the garden, and washed down with a middling South African Shiraz, were my supper. Christmas was imminent, I missed my people piercingly, but I felt that although I experienced omnipresent grief, life couldn't have been much better. A chili omelet, *à la* the Camellia Grill in New Orleans, Louisiana—actually better than I remember that touchstone chili omelet to be—on the night-before-Christmas Eve in Africa—well, I could never have imagined anything so rich.

CHURCHGOING IN MALAWI

ONE REASON I FELT AT home in Malawi was that the place reminded me of rural Louisiana at the time I was growing up there. Like Louisiana, Malawi was often hot and dusty, most of the people were black, life moved at a leisurely pace, and almost everyone went to church. The Presbyterian missionaries had done their work well, as had the Roman Catholics. People would ask without apology if you were Christian. I felt awkward answering that question, as I have been nominally an Episcopalian for most of my adult life but not much of a churchgoer. I embraced Christianity only in its broadest outlines.

I began attending St. Peter's, the little Anglican Church in Lilongwe, largely for sociological reasons. I thought I could understand the people better and get to know them if I went to services with them as religion was such a bedrock part of the culture.

Externally, the services seemed much the same as the ones I had always known, but three things seemed strikingly different in retrospect. One was the singing. Hearing Malawians sing in church wrings the heart. I never tried to sing any of the hymns, preferring just to listen to them. Their singing soared out of some mysterious place, spontaneous, unselfconscious, and unrehearsed. Their music seemed very complex, never done in the solid, mainline, foursquare Protestant way that most hymns are sung. They sang most of the standards, transforming them in the process to something rich and strange. They also sang "Kum Bah Yah, Lord," which delighted me because I had thought it was some white person's idea of a song Africans would sing.

While I didn't contribute to the singing, I did accept an invitation to read the Lesson of the Day on one or two occasions. I had one of those "I'm in Africa!" moments when I stood at the lectern and surveyed the all-black clergy and congregation. I wish I could report that I read well, but on the first occasion, I read from the wrong page. After the service, I apologized to the Rector, who said, "Don't worry. We like it when white people mess up. It makes us feel better." I believe I gave them several more opportunities to feel good after that.

The second striking thing was the flowers on the altar, hideous plastic things in garish colors now muted and faded. I puzzled over why these mere representations of flowers were used in a country in which poinsettias and other flowers grew riotously in the bush and on the sides of the road, free for anyone to gather. Perhaps the bush flowers, so ordinary and easily available, were considered vulgar, whereas the artificial ones were special—exotic and expensive, especially for a poor congregation. Maybe it was the Malawian equivalent of gold, frankincense, and myrrh or perhaps the Widow's Mite.

Finally, and most striking of all, was the sudden appearance of white people in church at Christmas and Easter services. In the two years I attended St. Peter's, I was often the only white person, *mzungu*, as we were called there, in the congregation. But at the High, Holy Days, many other whites descended on the tiny church, looking festive and unapologetic that they never came at any other time. They were always dressed up. I remember one handsome elderly man, resplendent in a white linen suit, boutonnière, cane, and spats. The women all wore fancy dresses and hats. I whispered to a woman who often sat next to me, "Who are these people?" "White people," she responded, "White people from the plantations."

I knew that the tea and coffee plantations were mostly owned and managed by expatriates who had lived in Malawi for many years, even generations. I knew only one other thing about them as a group, a disquieting fact. Volunteers said that the infant mortality rate among black children on the plantations was higher than in Malawi overall. I decided not to dwell on that fact whenever I saw them, but the thought invariably came to mind.

One amazing adventure I had was a trip to Mzuzu for the installation of the new Bishop. The Diocese of Malawi had recently been divided in half, and the powers that be in the Diocese of Northern Malawi called as their Bishop a man from Mississippi, a white man who had long been a priest in Malawi. I signed up to go to Mzuzu, seat of the New Diocese, for the installation ceremony. A bus was leaving from the church the following Saturday. When I arrived at the churchyard on the appointed day, people were milling about, but there was no bus to be seen. An hour later, the women, many with babies tied to their backs, had started to dance, the men were lounging about, but nothing else was happening. Someone who had been dispatched to find out about the bus returned an hour later with the news that it had been rented to some students for a trip to a sporting event. For the first time during that long day, I considered going home. Then three men were sent out to try to rent another bus. What seemed like hours later, actually only an hour and forty-five minutes, a bus rolled up, the women and girls stopped dancing, and everyone climbed aboard. It was now approaching noon.

We were about two hours into the trip that was said to require six or seven hours when the bus broke down. The people got off, undismayed, and sat down in a little grove of trees by the side of the road. By now, I was getting impatient, having invested five hours of my time. I fretted to Lucy, the Peace Corps nurse who was also on the trip. I said tentatively to her, "I could probably just go out to the road and flag down a ride and go back to Lilongwe." She replied, rather too quickly I thought, "Yes, why don't you do that?" I felt a little ashamed because no one else was fussing, planning an escape, or even showing signs of impatience. I realized that this was Africa, this was not unusual for them, and that from long experience, they had learned patience. I was being a typical white person, inwardly saying, "Let's go, let's go. What's the problem?" Clearly, to them, there was no problem, except for one high-strung *mzungu* in their midst. No wonder Lucy hoped I would bail out. I decided then and there that I would stick it out, no matter what.

Meanwhile, the women had pulled what food they had from their little hobo sacks. I shared the sumptuous lunch that Weston had prepared for the journey and was uneasy at its opulence compared to the meager provisions of my fellow parishioners. Later I was sorry to have given everything away; for by the time we reached Mzuzu, I was hungry, a condition with which my companions were no doubt familiar.

About two hours later, some men came and worked on the bus. When they pronounced it ready, we all climbed back on and set out for the north again. I started wondering what would happen if we didn't get to Mzuzu in time for the ceremony. It was scheduled for 10 the following morning. At the rate we had been going, it could very well have been over by the time we got there.

My fellow travelers sang for an hour or so, fell silent, then went to sleep. Among the passengers were five or six women with infants. I had already noted that they never cried. If they grew restless, the mothers gave them the breast immediately. I couldn't figure out how they managed the diaper issue. Later that night, because we were moving into the highlands of northern Malawi, the air became cooler, then a bit chilly. Around 11:00 we stopped to buy food at a roadside shack that sold roasted meat, probably goat, and bread. The owner also sold soft drinks, and almost everyone got a warm Coke or a Fanta, the national drink of Malawi. I only got out of the bus to stretch my legs and pee in the bushes with the other women, who had run off in the opposite direction from the men, presumably doing the same thing. Once back on the bus, I had the familiar feeling called "Are we there yet?"

We arrived in the small hours of the morning and were taken to a college dormitory to spend the rest of the night on mats on the floor. Lucy came to me before I had time to settle down and said that the other white people had arranged for me to stay in a different part of the school in a room that had regular beds. I protested that I preferred to remain with the group, but she insisted that I was expected and should go. I was too tired to argue and was led to the wing with small dorm rooms. I went to the assigned room and found one of the two beds occupied by a sleeping woman. I tried to undress and creep into the other bed without disturbing her, but she woke up and said, "Welcome. I'm Esther Miller." I would have preferred a room to myself, but as Peace Corps Volunteers had often told me, in Africa there was no privacy. Africans don't even want it, preferring to be together. Esther, it turned out, was an Anglican missionary with a long history in Malawi. I talked with her a lot during that weekend.

The next morning, far too early for me, I heard a great clamor of voices and the sound of doors being slammed, of women shouting to each other up and down the hall. Esther, who was already awake and dressed, sat calmly on the other bed reading the Bible. "What's all the noise?" I asked. "Just Africa waking up," she said. Africans wake up at first light. The concept of "sleeping in" after the first cockcrow was unknown in African life, so I got up, showered in the very basic and chilly common bathroom across the hall, and got dressed. In the dining room, we had tea and bread, then set out for the ceremony, which was being held in a football stadium across town.

I hadn't seen anyone from the bus since I arrived. I asked Esther where they might be and if I shouldn't join them. She told me that they understood and approved of the fact that I would be sitting with other VIPs in a special section. She said they would find that arrangement totally appropriate. It was expected. Once again, I acquiesced.

In the special seating section, church leaders and other dignitaries had plenty of time to talk, because the ceremony did not, of course, begin on time. In fact, it was hours late. I had time to study the crowd

near me. Many clergy in their collars and heavy
crosses, a few nuns, many dressed up people, both
black and white. Suddenly, a large group of women
appeared, all wearing a uniform of sorts with the
special *tchinge* designed for the occasion. One woman
carried a placard aloft announcing their home parish
in Zambia. Following them came another group,
wearing identical *tchinges*, from a parish in Tanzania.
The magnitude of the event hadn't struck me until
that moment. The faithful had come from all over
Malawi and southern Africa for the occasion. After a
seemingly endless parade of women's groups, the
Bishop and his retinue entered the stadium amid the
cheers and applause of the faithful. He was at this
point just a small figure on the field, dwarfed by the
cheering crowds. He acknowledged the applause for
some time, then began circumnavigating the field,
blessing the people. Eventually, he mounted the stage
and the ceremony of his installation took place. After
the ceremony, he took to the field once more, blessing
the people and acknowledging their good wishes.

After the ceremony, I was shepherded, along with
many others in the grandstand, to a church where tea
and a supper were provided. There I met and shook
the hand of the new Bishop. When I told him I was
from Louisiana, he expressed his happiness to meet a
fellow southerner and his satisfaction with the Peace
Corps Volunteers, many of whom he had met over the
years. He seemed to me a kind of old-fashioned
gentleman of the South, very kind and approachable.
He asked me if I knew a certain Louisiana family and
offered that they were "lovely people." But this was
not a man content with idle social chatter. He told me
that he wanted to establish the seat of the new Diocese
on Likoma Island, in the middle of Lake Malawi. The
missionaries had settled there and built a cathedral in
the early nineteenth century. I said I thought it would

be a daunting task, as the island was quite inaccessible—three days by boat—and the cathedral from what I had heard, was in very bad repair. He recognized that but said if the people wanted to do it, he would make it a priority.

On the Tuesday following the installation, the Bishop appeared unannounced in my office, just to say hello and to thank me for attending the ceremony. He asked if there were Volunteers on the island. There was only one at that time, but we had a Volunteer at another site who was an architect. The Bishop invited us to come to Likoma as his guests so she could look at the church and its outbuildings and draw plans. He suggested that we plan to come over on the Ilala, a steamship that sails around the lake. I remarked to myself that he wasn't wasting any time launching his new agenda. When the time came I was not able to make the trip, but the young architect did, and she reported that she had begun working on the plans.

Another meeting took place on that trip to Mzuzu that I still remember vividly. Esther introduced me to a priest named John, a native of New Zealand who had been a priest in Africa for most of his life. As a young man, he had been one of the first white members of the African National Congress and had come under pressure from the government and others. He wore a black leather glove on his right hand, which Esther had already told me, had been blown off by a letter bomb. I was drawn to him for his moral clarity and courage.

During our conversation that night he told me about the early days of the ANC. He also talked a little about his accident. Apparently, his hand was so badly injured that he was sent to London for treatment. Both Nelson Mandela and Desmond Tutu visited him in the hospital there. I asked him if he was married. "No," he said, a little sadly, I thought. "I never felt I could subject a woman to the dangers she would face with me. I was always a marked man." At this time, he was the Bishop Designee for Northern Zambia and was to be installed several months hence. He invited me to come to the ceremony, but once again, the pressure of my duties interfered.

Later that evening, we went back to the college for the night. I still hadn't seen anyone from the bus, but there was a note telling me to be ready at 6 because the bus would "come pick me," as they say in Malawi. I wanted to see Esther again and learn more about her work, but I never did. All the do-gooders in Malawi were kept busy because there was so much good that needed doing.

During the trip home, I made an avoidable mistake that caused me some frustration. I looked at my watch and calculated that I would be home in eight hours or around 2 in the afternoon, perhaps 3 because this was Africa. Weston would have my supper ready; I could hunker down with Katie for the evening, and go to bed early. O Foolish Woman! We actually arrived past 10.

During the trip, I witnessed a curious phenomenon—roadside shopping. First, the bus stopped so people could buy firewood, which they piled up in front of the door. After that, at every stop, and there would be many, the wood had to be removed so people could get out and then replaced before the bus could start up again. People wanted to stop for vegetables, for meat, for anything they could afford that was cheaper outside the capital. I could not find that place of peace and contentment with which I had begun the trip.

All I wanted now was to be in my own bed, so each stop was agony. I did not want to communicate my impatience to others who seemed to be having a fine time. I tried to calm myself by watching the countryside of northern Malawi go by. Once it grew dark, the bus settled down. There were several pee-and-Fanta stops, but it began to seem as thought we might actually get back to Lilongwe that night. We finally arrived after midnight. Our progress was slowed because there were people on the bus who had requested to be dropped off. In order to accommodate them, we probably went miles off the direct route. I tried to sleep and put it out of my mind.

My resistance to the pace of things wore me out, and by the time I arrived back home I was thoroughly exhausted. It was beginning to dawn on me that if I were to survive in Africa, I would need to have a serious attitude adjustment.

Tiring though it was, the trip was a success. In retrospect, the trip to the north was time well spent because I learned so many things about the country, the people, their faith, their kindness to me, and their talent for making life in Africa bearable if not downright fun.

MONKEYS AND BABOONS AT CAPE MACLEAR

MONKEYS AND BABOONS LIVE LARGE in my memories of Malawi. I once went to this area to visit staff members in a remote post at the southern end of Lake Malawi. The trip promised to be exciting because we would stay a day or two in Lake Malawi National Park at Cape Maclear, a freshwater aquatic park. The park was notable for its astonishing natural beauty and was also home to the *cichlid*, the brilliantly colored little fish sold in the States and elsewhere to aquarium enthusiasts. These freshwater fish, known to aquarists as *Mbuna*, exist in Lake Malawi and nowhere else.

Ninety species of *Mbuna* were protected at the park, and perhaps a hundred other species exist outside the protected area.

Dr. Livingston explored this part of the lake and named the Cape after his friend and personal physician, a fellow Scot named Stuart Maclear. The Cape was well known to backpackers and other visitors in Africa for its beautiful beaches, breathtaking sunsets, and plentiful supplies of relatively inexpensive supplies of Malawi Gold.

The bay was ringed with steep green hills all around and dominated by a mountain thrusting up from the water to a height of 500 meters. The water at the Cape was the clearest I'd ever seen. I was told that because visitors often fed the fish, they were not afraid of people and would follow swimmers, hoping for a handout. I wanted to snorkel there, but the threat of getting schistosomiasis had to be considered. "Shisto" only got nasty if left untreated, and the treatment, a handful of pills with no side effects, was benign. I probably already had schistosomiasis because I swam in the Lake at The Livingstonia Hotel all the time. But at Salima, where the hotel was located, this disease was not endemic. At Monkey Bay, that was not the story. One had to deal with the likelihood of getting it —"You go in the water; you've got shisto"—a doctor friend told me. I decided to pass. I didn't feel like taking any more pills than I already did; and besides, I could see the fish from the glass bottom boat.

As the driver Salim pulled into Monkey Bay, I said, "I hope I see a monkey while I'm here." He laughed and pointed up ahead. Monkeys and baboons were everywhere I looked—in the trees, on the grounds, on the roofs of the buildings. I had seen a monkey on the road into the park. A young boy in shorts was holding it up by its tail. The monkey was arching its back and looking at our car with its bright eyes. Salim explained that the boy was trying to sell it. "For a pet?" I asked. "No, Madam, to eat." I wasn't prepared for that answer, and I felt sick and sad to think about it. How could anyone eat these lovely, clever, and mischievous little creatures? I remembered an awful thing I had heard about poachers killing the gorillas in Rwanda to get their hands. They made ashtrays of them for the tourist trade!

A FLOCK OF
PIGEONS

OURS WEREN'T THE SHOWY WHITE kind with tails like
ruffled fans, the kind Picasso and Matisse made into a
cliché image of southern France. Ours were the
common ones found in every African village and even
in the back yards of city dwellings. Dingy birds, tan or
gray mixed with white, they seemed dull in a
landscape of tropical birds, flame trees, and
poinsettias growing wild in the bush.

One day while sitting on the veranda (or *khande*,
as they called it in southern Africa) about the time the
shadows fell on Mt. Mulanje, I watched the
homecoming of my neighbor's flock. Two or three at a
time, they flew in, circled, then touched down. One
could see this sight all over Malawi in the late

afternoon. Nearly every family kept pigeons to supplement their food supply. They were flying protein.

I had no interest in pigeons as food, but I came to love seeing them winging home night after night. I started thinking about getting a flock too. "Weston," I said not long after, "I think I'd like some pigeons." He began to tell me that he could get them at the market the next morning and prepare them for dinner. How many guests would I be having?

"No, no," I said. "I just want some to watch." He looked mildly surprised, and I was mildly embarrassed. In a country where so many people were just one step ahead of serious hunger, it seemed frivolous to say I wanted them for my pleasure. He was probably thinking, "These crazy *azungu*! What next?"

Then an idea formed as I was speaking it. "Weston, if you take care of the flock now, I will give them to you when I leave. When I've gone, you can do with them as you like." He said, "Don't worry, Madam. I will see to them."

The very next day, Weston and Maki, the garden boy, went to the market to buy the materials to build a pigeonniere. With Weston supervising and Maki doing the construction, the little pigeon house was up on its pole in the middle of the back garden by nightfall. It must have been a traditional design because it looked like all the other pigeon houses I had seen, down to the umbrella-shaped roof and the rickety ladder leading up to the door. All we needed now were the birds.

When Weston and Maki returned from the market with six birds in a crate on the back of the bicycle, I peeked inside to see them. Six pairs of startled and startling red eyes stared back. Weston scattered grain at the base of the pole while Maki

stood on the ladder and stuffed straw into the house.
Weston kept the birds in the crate for several days,
feeding them every morning and evening. Then he put
them into the house and shut them up at the time
when the birds usually fly home and tuck up for the
night.

The next morning, the entire household
assembled to witness their release. Miriam, Weston's
wife, stood with the children, who were dressed in
their school uniforms. Even the day guard, Wilson,
who had just reported for duty, was present for the
historic occasion. The birds came out, one by one,
perched on the little sill, and flapped off without a
backward glance. I wondered if we would see them
again.

The workday seemed endless because I was in a
fever of anticipation to get home to await the arrival of
the flock. We waited, Weston, Miriam, and the
children, on the *khande*. Maki had gone for the day by
this time, but Wison (not to be confused with Wilson),
the night guard, watched the skies from his post at the
gate.

The pigeons next door were already coming in,
but ours were nowhere to be seen. We waited an
agonizing fifteen minutes more. When Wison spotted
the first one winging in, he shouted, "Madam, they are
coming home." A lone bird, a gray one, circled and
landed briskly and began pecking the grain at the foot
of the pole. I was worried about the rest but two more,
then a third arrived and landed.

When it became apparent that no more were
coming, Weston said, "Don't worry, Madam. They
have gone back to the market. I will fetch them home
in the morning."

Early the next day, the lady next door sent her
gardener to say that her flock had returned,
accompanied by a strange bird. Weston went for it

and brought it back. That evening, the pigeon failed to return; so Weston retrieved it again and shut it up in the crate. At pigeon bedtime, he put it up with its fellows. The following evening, it came home with the rest of the flock.

By now, it was clear that we had lost one. A check of the market and a visit to the neighbor proved fruitless. Weston was philosophical. "A cat, probably." I took care not to register too much disappointment. Malawi had, after all, one of the highest infant mortality rates in the world, and I thought that excessive concern over a pigeon would be unseemly. And, I concluded, five out of six ain't bad.

We never replaced the one that was lost and continued with a flock of five until the pigeons began their family. Because the pigeonniere was high up on the pole, we couldn't see from the ground if their constant courtship activities had produced results.

When Weston reported that there were eggs in the nest, I wanted to know how many. Weston said we shouldn't disturb them at this critical stage. I had many unanswered questions. Were all the hens laying? How many hens did we have? Did the whole flock go out every day, or did one or more stay back to sit on the nest?

One day Maki reported that he had heard "chip chipping" from above, but Weston would not let anyone go up to see. A week or so later, he crept up the precarious steps to investigate. He came back down and announced, "There are six."

About a week later, I was sitting on the *khande* after lunch with Katie sleeping at my feet when suddenly she bounded off the porch and into the garden. I didn't see the chick fall from the nest but she obviously had. Katie, the Silver Streak, killed it in one swift motion and began carrying it around the garden in her mouth, looking proud of herself. She didn't maul it or try to eat it. I was annoyed with her until I remembered that Weimaraners were bird dogs; she had done as her nature required.

I called for Weston. He took in the situation in a glance. He patted Katie on the head, and she dropped the tiny naked thing at his feet. He picked it up and said the children would bury it when they came home from school, which they did with all due ceremony but no discernible grief. They were used to death.

There were no more calamities after that. The babies learned to fly and were soon coming and going with the flock. More little ones hatched, and the pigeons were in continuous production mode after that. I lost track of how many we had, but Weston always knew and could report the number immediately if I asked.

Six or eight months later, not long before my term of service was scheduled to end, I was obliged to move to new quarters because the Indian gentleman who owned the house I lived in wanted to sell it. I hated to leave because I was happy where I was and moving meant that Weston and his family would be dislocated. The children were settled in their school and would have to transfer to a new one.

Another perturbing thing was that my successor had written to say that she did not intend to employ Weston. She didn't want a man with a family on the place. She preferred a single woman. When I told Weston the disappointing news, he said, "Don't worry, Madam. I will find another situation." He asked if in the meantime, he could move the pigeons to his brother's village. I had hoped that my successor would move into the house, continue to employ Weston, and allow him and his family to stay on the place. I assumed that the pigeons would remain there too. Nothing would change. Like so many of my schemes to make life better for the Africans I came to admire and love, it was not to be.

Weston and Maki captured the pigeons the next morning and put them into a crate, packed up the pigeon house, the stairs, and the pole, and took them to the village where Weston's brother lived. The brother was happy enough to be their custodian because Weston had agreed to share the eggs.

The night before the pigeonniere was to be dismantled, I sat on the *khande* one last time and watched the flock swoop home through the amethyst twilight. Weston shut them in their little house where they would stay until the brother came with a truck to take them away. Early in the morning, he climbed back up the steps with a small cardboard box and extracted a pair to give to Maki.

I was surprised at how desolate I was to see them go. They would be well cared for, and I was happy to be making Weston a pigeon baron. And surely I wasn't attached to those birds. I hadn't tended them, hadn't named any of them, and can't see any of them clearly as I write this years later.

I realized later that I was grieving for a time of peace and comfort when I could sit and enjoy the lawn and the flame trees and the frangipani. I could forget the frustrations and uncertainties of the day and throw a ball to Katie, who never missed, not even once. The pigeons captured the essence of these brief periods of repose at day's end. Their soaring flight home every evening meant that I was home too. I had made a home of a rented house, tacky government-issue furniture, a flock of village pigeons, and a servant and his family. The sense of being at home that I felt during those evenings on the *khande* was an unexpected blessing. I never experienced it again in Africa.

I didn't cry when the pigeons were driven away in Weston's brother's borrowed truck, or later when I said goodbye to Weston, to Miriam and the children, to Maki and Katie. I was rational about the whole thing, knowing that I had come for a limited time and would be leaving. I protected myself from the pain of good-bye. But now, I cry while writing, while reading over what I've written, while looking at pictures of those beautiful African faces, especially those of the sturdy African men who knew how to do everything, even pretend that a flock of pigeons was cause for great excitement. When I feel really sad and my memories of them tear at my heart, I sometimes hear Weston say, "Don't worry, Madam. Everything will be all right."

THE BLOODY BABE

ONE THING I REMEMBERED ABOUT Africa with startling clarity was the closeness I felt to the foundation stones of life—birth and death. Before Africa, I had been to many baptisms and funerals, but never had I been fully present when a person first took breath or breathed the last. Both of my parents died while I was away. My father, I was told, passed willingly and peacefully in his late eighties; my mother fought like a wildcat to hang on to her bare scrap of life before she succumbed in her early nineties.

I myself bore three children, two of whom survived. In all three cases, I was in a drug-induced state when they were born—it was the fifties, a time when doctors delivered the babies, not the mothers. I had read Grantley Dick Read, but when I broached the subject of natural childbirth with my obstetrician, he

snorted and said that wasn't realistic and that he
would be reluctant to manage such a case. "We're not
Indians," he said. "Why go backwards?" So I don't
remember much about the birth of my beautiful
daughter, but I distinctly recall the doctor telling the
nurse; "I'm going to check on some other things. I'll
deliver in about forty-five minutes." I suppose I could
have resisted this doc-centered approach, this
"managed childbirth," I think it was called; but I was
barely twenty years old at the time and accustomed to
following orders from men.

When my second child was born, I vaguely
remembered the doctor announcing that the baby he
had just "delivered" was "a big, beautiful boy." He was
born on a Friday and would be dead by Sunday. I had
a brief glimpse of him and never saw him again. Once
in my room and more or less awake, I asked for the
baby. The nurses gave evasive responses. Later, I was
told that the he was having trouble breathing and that
a specialist from New Orleans was on his way. It was
strongly suggested that I stay in bed; so when my
firstborn son died, it was my brave husband who kept
the watch and attended the funeral with my father
and mother.

When my third child came some years later, the
same doctor delivered in the same way. Once again, I
brought a child into the world without being fully
present. Happily, he was a big "thriver," and that
would be the end of my personal brush with life and
death in childbirth. It seems to me now that those
events took place somewhere else and happened to
someone else. Those important occurrences of my life
seemed to take place offstage, something I have since
regretted.

I understood that in Africa, especially in
underdeveloped countries, people were frequently
confronted with both birth and death; and while I

wasn't seeking those experiences, I assumed they would probably be part of my life there. Curiously, they were not. Many of the Peace Corps Volunteers dealt directly with these events and some even participated, being much closer to the ground than I was. I often talked with them when they came to the office, to assure myself that these powerful events had not left them troubled. Usually, they took their brushes with both life and death in stride. One young man told me a story about the death he had just witnessed. An old man in his village died slowly. The Volunteer took turns with the villagers who fanned the dying one in shifts over a period of four days and nights. "In Africa," he said, "No one dies alone."

As for births, they happened often in bush villages, but I never witnessed an actual delivery. I came closest to a birth one day while visiting Volunteers in the bush when I went for a walkabout and met Gail on the path. She told me that she was just coming from a birth. I didn't ask her if she had attended because I knew she had, even though health sector Volunteers were strictly forbidden to deliver babies, the result of some litigation issue, I suppose. The Peace Corps had recently announced unenforceable orders that the Volunteers should only give health lessons to the women and train midwives. They were also encouraged to give out little midwifery kits containing a ball of twine, a pair of scissors, and a pair of rubber gloves.

I knew from the beginning that these were orders made to be disobeyed, or at least ignored. I immediately decided not to make this an issue with the Volunteers. However, I was obliged to inform them of the policy. The women, many of whom had already assisted in several, perhaps many births, were incredulous. One of them challenged me directly, demanding, "If you were alone with a woman in hard labor, minutes from delivering her baby, what would you do? Would you catch it or not?" I replied that I would follow my conscience and be willing to take the consequences, if any occurred.

When Gail asked me if I wanted to greet the new mother and child, the answer was "Of course." Anytime a Volunteer wanted me to see their field, meet the Village headman, or tour the clinic they were building, the answer was an automatic and enthusiastic "yes." Although I was genuinely interested in them and their projects, I must admit that tramping through the bush after driving for hundreds of miles in 100+ heat made me wish I could just buy them all a beer and call it a day.

"Are you sure the Amayie will want to see a stranger so soon?" I asked. She replied, "If my Big comes to greet her, she will be so honored that she will probably name the baby after you. The kid will be remembered as the girl Gail's Big saw on her birthday." With that, I followed her back to a tiny shack, empty of furniture except for a cot and a mat. The new mother, looking rather dazed and rubbing her abdomen, sat on the floor. The infant, wrapped in a piece of colored cloth, lay on the cot. Gail introduced me to the mother and explained that I had come to congratulate her and greet the new one. The woman looked at me, smiling shyly, and nodded her head.

Gail picked up the little lump from the cot and let the fabric fall away, revealing the thirty-minute-old child in all her naked glory, and handed her to me. She was still sticky. Gail had wiped her down but not washed her. " Her pains came on her fast and hard. There was no time to go for water." The tiny girl began squirming and mewing. I held her awkwardly for a few more minutes, then Gail held out the cloth to receive her. I held her close. Bless you, Sweet Babe, I thought. She screwed up her wizened little face and let out a thin wail. I wanted to celebrate her entrance into this world, but I was suddenly overcome with sadness, knowing that her chances to live and thrive were not good. Judging from her mother's circumstances, she would grow up poor, perhaps die in infancy of malnutrition, or later of malaria, or worst of all in childbirth. I didn't want Amayie to see my grief, so I smiled when I shook her hand, wished her well, and congratulated her on her accomplishment.

I watched Gail swaddle up the baby expertly and return her to the cot. I said to her, also to cover my sorrow and not appear to be a sniveler before a Volunteer, "You seem pretty comfortable with all this."

"I should be," she said. "I'm a registered nurse and a certified midwife."

"I remember," I said. " Will this baby live?" I asked.

She frowned and then replied gently, "The odds aren't good. She's underweight, the mother's not healthy, the conditions aren't favorable, and she's miles from a clinic."

I didn't see Gail until her next trip to town some three months later. She came into the office to see me and after shaking my hand, did not let it go. She told me gently that the baby had not survived her first six weeks. "It was the bloody diarrhea. We've been seeing a lot of that lately. It's the season."

"And Amayie? "

"She is very sad. It was her first." She hugged me hard and then went about her business.

O Africa, I thought. What a hard place you are, and a mystery. In spite of the number of deaths—not only from childbirth, but also from AIDS, malaria, dysentery, complications of malnutrition, and other causes—the country was teeming with life. Nearly every woman I saw had a baby on her back or at her breast. Most women, even the ones with infants, were pregnant as well. Infertility, the treatment of which was a growth industry in the States, was not a problem.

The animals, too, were always in the reproductive mode. Driving along the roads and in the game parks, one saw pregnant females everywhere and numerous cubs, pups, chicks, calves, etc. Plant life was vigorous. The rich soil, the color of used coffee grounds, would support almost any kind of plant growth, and the very air smelled intensely organic, the recognizable smell of generation. Fecundity in Africa was palpable.

It was as though everything was wildly speeded up. An insane, out-of-control, explosive outcropping of life, together with an insane, out-of-control, explosive eruption of morbidity and mortality. "The force that drives the green fuse," as Dylan Thomas called the life force, drives harder in Africa and creates both life and death with ever more velocity.

THANKSGIVING IN MALAWI

I PARTICIPATED IN TWO THANKSGIVING observances one year. Our medical people, Fred and Wendy, had Thanksgiving dinner at their house on Thursday. I was the duty officer until noon, but they weren't planning to serve until around 3 p.m., so I got there in plenty of time. They had turkey with all the trimmings. About twelve people sat down to dinner. No one gave thanks; no one mentioned absent family; everyone simply "fell to." The conversation centered on where the food came from, a constant topic of interest to Peace Corps workers in Africa. One hears such conversations at every table: "Where did you find these shrimp?" "Mozzarella cheese! Where did you get it? South Africa? Damn! I want some for my dinner party on Friday." Everyone lusts after delicacies that were generally unavailable. I was still satisfied with the local abundance, but I predicted I would fall into this way of thinking and talking too. "Mzuzu coffee! Let's place a big order. Count me in."

The second observance of Thanksgiving took place at the Ntchisi Forest Rest House, an old Colonial structure, probably once a hunting lodge, in the middle of Ntchisi Forest.

One of the Volunteers, an extraordinary guy who looked like the young Baryshnikov and was a serious cook, had thirty people come to the park, which was near his site, for an overnight occasion on the weekend after Thanksgiving. He procured and cooked four turkeys with stuffing and all the other accoutrements we associate with the day. The guy, unlike most of the Volunteers, was upper crust. The Peace Corps, being an essentially middle-class expression, has few such people. He came from the West Coast, where his father was a broker and his mother was once a Vogue model, as was his grandmother. He prepped at Lawrenceville and went to Harvard.

At his little house, which we visited on the way up the mountain, he had installed a beautiful terrace and planted a large garden with herbs and flowers in addition to the usual vegetables. He also covered his tacky furniture in cowhide (bought in the local market) and hung the skull, which he bleached, above his fireplace. On his mantel were pictures of his beautiful and classy-looking family. He had a certain natural sense of style.

The conversation at this party had nothing to do with where he got the food but centered instead on liquor. "Is there any more of that Jack Daniels?" and "Pass the whiskey." The Volunteers seemed to have college drinking habits, and most of the guests appeared to be quite intoxicated as the day wore on. They stumbled around playing football and Frisbee before settling down to some serious drinking after dinner.

I was ready to go home right after the meal, but since I had driven a vehicle full of Volunteers for three hours up the mountain and would have to drive them down again the next morning, there was no escape. I went into my cocoon mode around 7:30 p.m. After I had been asleep for about an hour and a half, Paul and Gigi, whose room I was sharing, woke me up to see the rain. It was pelting down, and the thunder and lightning display was "awesome." People were sitting on the veranda, getting drunker and drunker now; and they cheered after each pyrotechnical outburst. It was something like watching fireworks on the 4th of July—"Ooh, aha, that was a big one. Aww right!" The wind came up, and the rain blowing onto the veranda was cold. I went back to bed, and when I woke up around 3, only the hard core was still in evidence. I devoted a few minutes to worrying about sliding down the mountain on muddy roads with a carful of drunks, but that concern wasn't enough to keep me awake. I had learned to detach in the midst of crowds. If you wanted privacy, close your eyes.

CHRISTMAS CAME
A LITTLE LATE

OF MY SIX CHRISTMASES IN AFRICA, the one I remember most vividly was my first in Niger, the Christmas I thought wasn't taking place.

In an overwhelmingly Muslim country like Niger, Christmas was not heralded by the imagery of the northern hemisphere—the fir trees, the holly and the ivy, Rudolph and Frosty. No jingle bells or ho, ho, ho, no fake or real snow, no seasonal specialties and holiday wines and spirits in the market. In Africa, even Christian countries like Malawi were too poor for such excesses. Poverty enforces a certain purity; and attempts by expatriates to introduce the standard symbols at their holiday parties always seemed to me to fall a little flat, merely calling attention to the

absence of both the good and the bad aspects of
Christmas.

Ironically, in Niger, a country in which Christmas
scarcely exists, the images of the first Christmas, so
blunted and debased in America by commercialism,
can be seen everywhere in North Africa. If the citizens
of Niamey wanted to stage a Living Nativity, it
wouldn't take long to assemble the props or the
costumes. No cow shed with a straw roof would have
to be constructed, nobody's mother would have to
stitch up cloaks and turbans, no sheep and goats
would need to be trucked in from a nearby farm.
Many women even today wear the garments we
associate with the Virgin, a long, simple dress with a
big scarf covering the head and shoulders. One sees
plenty of men who could play shepherds because they
were shepherds, wearing the rough garments, rope
belts, and sandals that American moms must
improvise for their little pageant actors. Everything
necessary for a Nativity reenactment in Niamey was
richly and readily available on the streets of the town.

The few Christian churches in Niamey, with the
possible exception of the Roman Catholic Cathedral,
did not seem to emphasize the holiday. Even there,
the approach seemed rather casual. I remember
driving through town on that Christmas Eve afternoon
with the American Ambassador's wife. She asked her
chauffeur to drive by the Cathedral so she could
inquire about the times of Christmas Eve masses, as
she and Excellence were thinking of attending. We
pulled up at the imposing structure, went into the
reception, and asked the young woman at the desk for
the schedule of Christmas masses. She looked puzzled
and said she didn't have one: we would have to ask
Pere Bonnard for those details. We hunted down a
sleepy little French priest who also told us he wasn't
sure about the times. He rummaged around on his

desk and produced a scrap of paper that said
Midnight Mass, 11 p.m.

I went to Mass that night and found it an
interesting cultural event but not a worshipful one, at
least not for me. I was too fascinated by the theatrical
elements. Nigérienne women and girls danced up the
aisles and presented themselves at the crèche just to
the right of the central aisle. Mary and Joseph
followed, walking slowly. Mary sat down by the crèche
with Joseph standing beside her. When someone
stepped out and proclaimed the birth of the Savior,
the Bishop, an imposing Frenchman, appeared with a
baby in his arms and held it aloft. And said
commandingly, "*Regardez*" It was, I must say, a
thrilling moment. As he walked up and down the aisle
holding the baby above his head, he passed by my
place on the aisle, and I saw a tiny brown arm
dangling limply from the blanket. When he returned
the baby to the Virgin, she took it and put it into the
cradle. It looked lifeless and never stirred or made a
peep for the duration of the service. I decided it must
be a doll. "*Poupee*?" I whispered to the man sitting
next to me. "*Mais, non*," he replied, "*c'est un bel
enfant.*" I concluded that if it were a real baby, it had
been drugged for the occasion, an unsettling thought.

I went the next day to dinner at the home of the
American Deputy Chief of Mission. He and his
Australian wife served a lovely repast, with many
dishes on the buffet, each accompanied by a card
announcing what it was. The meal was a greatly
expanded version of the traditional American holiday
feast, but nothing else acknowledged that it was
Christmas—no reference to it as we sat down to eat,
no Christmas toast when the champagne was poured,
no Christmas blessing. No children running around
saying, "He broke my truck," or "This thing doesn't
have any batteries," or "Can I have my pie now?" I

went home feeling out of joint and thinking that for the second night in a row, Christmas had passed me by.

The next morning, I left for the office before sunrise, relieved to put The Christmas That Never Was behind me. The town was mostly deserted, and the dust of the *Harmattan* had turned the sky an unimaginable shade of salmon. I drove through the dawn along the wide boulevards lined with palms, the kind of avenues the French colonials built wherever they went. When I saw on my left three men on camels, not an uncommon sight on the streets of Niamey, I stopped the car to let them cross. Only as they passed directly in front of me did I see them clearly. Two looked like light-skinned Arabs or *Tuaregs*, the third was a black African. All were majestic in full desert regalia. The image suddenly took my breath. "Ah," I thought, "Exit the Kings."

THE COLOR OF A LION'S EYE

NOT EVERY PEACE CORPS PROJECT was of equal interest and excitement. That was not to say that the less interesting ones didn't need doing. Many were vital. But some projects stand out in my memory, even over the passage of years. I played a brief but terrifying role in one of the more memorable ones—the visit of the veterinarians.

The Volunteers in Niger were distressed at the deplorable condition of the animals in the public zoo in the capital city. Being "can do" people, they made contact with a veterinarian in the States who was interested in wild animal treatment. It was arranged that he and a team would come to Niger to visit the appalling zoo maintained (or not) by the city of

Niamey.

I don't know how or why the *Le Jardin Zoologique* was founded. Perhaps it was a noble effort at educating the local people in biology, hoping to generate respect for the creatures that shared their lands. I had my doubts about the zoo in Niger, among the poorest countries in Africa, if not the world. How could the people afford a zoo when so many of them were undernourished themselves? When a monkey could make a meal and a wild boar feed a family?

The doctor proposed to bring a team of both large and small animal vets and technicians to diagnose and treat the long-neglected captives, to oversee the cleanup and repairs to the physical facility, and to train some Nigériens to continue the work. I was particularly concerned about the sustainability of the project. What permanent good would it do if we couldn't leave behind a group of local people sufficiently trained, resourced, and motivated to carry on the work? I had heard former Volunteers say how disappointed they were to return to their sites and find the clinic they built, the library they created and stocked with books, the wells they dug no longer in use. The problem of sustainability was not just related to physical structures although Africa was a place where things crumbled, got overgrown, rusted out quickly. It was also a place where people forgot. In one sad case I heard of, the man whom the Volunteer had taught to maintain the pump for the well he dug had died, and no one else in the village knew how to do it. So the women were back on the roads carrying jugs of water on their heads.

A former Volunteer once told me that during her three-year stint, she had seen a guinea worm-infested village cure itself by the simple act of filtering the drinking water. All that was required was a net of some sort—a stocking or piece of fabric placed over the neck of the jugs to filter out the guinea-worm larvae and thus break the cycle of guinea-worm infestation. The prevention was so simple and the failure to prevent so devastating (the larvae travel through the bloodstream, develop into worms which end up in the feet, and finally burst out through the skin.) When people have Guinea worm, their feet swell and become infected, rendering them unable to work or go to school.

The Volunteer went from village to village distributing nets, demonstrating their use and stressing their importance. When she revisited formerly Guinea Worm-free villages, she would often find a recurrence of the scourge. She told me that she had been discouraged to learn that the villagers had forgotten to use the nets or hadn't replaced the ones they had been given, even with readily available pieces of cloth. I was disheartened too; then we reminded ourselves that it had taken over forty years for the "Smoking kills" message to take hold in the United States, and that even today many people there still smoke. Others didn't take medications responsibly and were not compliant with the simplest instructions. It wasn't just an African thing but rather a human problem.

My job as Directrice was to meet and greet the team, have them over for dinner, and be available to them if problems should arise. They had arrived at a particularly busy time in the *bureau*, so after the formalities, I turned my attention to other matters.

A couple of days later, the head vet sent word informing me that on the following morning, he and his team expected to begin treating the big cats and invited me to visit the site. I made plans to attend, of course. I assumed that I would be watching the proceedings from a safe distance, but the party chief had other ideas. He explained that he would be injecting the lions with anesthesia. After they were down, it would be perfectly safe for me to step into the cage and see them up close, even touch them.

I thanked him and said I would be there. I was not driven by the need to see and touch huge beasts in close quarters, but by the knowledge that if I showed fear, the Volunteers would not respect me and would question my fitness to lead them. The vet would "dart" his first large patient, a female, around 9 a.m., so I arrived earlier to greet the party and the Volunteers from the project.

The lioness was pacing around the cage, looking warily at the doctor as he approached the cage with the dart gun in hand. When he shot, she gave no sign of having felt anything; but shortly after, she began to stagger in a circle, foaming heavily at the mouth, round and round a few times until she dropped. The doctor entered the cage and approached her confidently. He checked her pulse. When he dropped her foot, it fell heavily onto the concrete floor. "She's out," he announced. "Now you can come in and have a look."

In moments like this, I always asked myself a question: Would I rather die like this, or would I prefer to die drooling and babbling in a wheelchair? Being mauled by a lion in Africa seemed infinitely more interesting than drooling and babbling. I stepped quickly into the cage.

"You can touch her," he said, "assuming that I would want to.

I put my hand on her neck and patted gingerly. The vet reached over and took her shaggy head in his hands. "Look," he said, "inside her eyes." He held the lids open as I moved in closer. Deep inside, I saw a miraculous color—a pure, cold green, the color of the inside of a kiwi. I was seized by the moment and could not take my eyes away. My memory, uninvited, supplied an image—*From Greenland's Icy Mountains*, a line I learned as a child from a pompous and condescending Anglican missionary hymn I had not thought of in decades. I had seen something I had not, in my strangest dream, ever expected to see. That color, which I can still recall, came to stand for the mystery of Africa, and the mystery of my life that had brought me to this beautiful and terrible place. I sat back. The doctor asked if I wanted to look again. I shook my head no. I had come, I had seen, and I would never forget.

Biography

Jane F. Bonin was born in deepest Louisiana. After marrying a successful lawyer, and while bringing up two children, she earned a Ph.D. in English and won The Distinguished Professor Award at the University of Louisiana in Lafayette, Louisiana. Always a writer, she published three books of drama history and criticism as well as some thirty reviews and critical articles during this period. After retiring from the university, she relocated to Washington, D.C., and took a job with the US State Department on the staff of the Foreign Service Institute. In 1964, she accepted a position on the Peace Corps staff in Africa, first in Malawi for two years and then in Niger as Country Director for four. During her time in Africa, she began to write in a more personal way about her life there. *The Color of A Lion's Eye* contains vignettes covering her experiences in the difficult places she came to love. Today, she devotes her attention to reading and writing, both in French and English, and to singing in a large chorale. She enjoys the cultural riches of Washington, especially its many museums and theaters.